BATHROOM REMODELING

D0826292

BUILDER-TESTED │ CODE APPROVED

BATHROOM REMODELING

FROM THE EDITORS OF **Fine Homebuilding**

The Taunton Press

© 2011 by the Taunton Press, Inc.
Photographs © 2011 by the Taunton Press, Inc., except where noted
All rights reserved.

The Taunton Press
Inspiration for hands-on living®

The Taunton Press Inc., 63 South Main St., PO Box 5506, Newtown, CT 06470-5506
e-mail: tp@taunton.com

Editor: Alex Giannini
Copy editor: Candace B. Levy
Technical editor: Dave Yates
Indexer: Jay Kreider
Cover design: Alexander Isley, Inc.
Interior design and layout: Cathy Cassidy
Front cover photographer: Roe A. Osborn, courtesy *Fine Homebuilding* magazine © The Taunton Press, Inc.
Back cover photographer: Justin Fink, courtesy *Fine Homebuilding* magazine © The Taunton Press, Inc.

Taunton's For Pros By Pros® and *Fine Homebuilding®* are trademarks of The Taunton Press Inc., registered in the U.S. Patent and Trademark Office.

Library of Congress Cataloging-in-Publication Data

Bathroom remodeling / from the editors of Fine Homebuilding.
    p. cm.
  Includes index.
  ISBN 978-1-60085-363-0
  1. Bathrooms--Remodeling. I. Fine homebuilding.
  TH4816.3.B37B382 2011
  643'.520288--dc22

                    2011006942

Printed in the United States of America
10 9 8 7 6 5 4 3 2 1

The following manufacturers/names appearing in *Bathroom Remodeling* are trademarks: American Standard® Ceramix®, American Standard Champion 4®, Aqua Glass®, Aqua-Tough™, Aquia®, Architectural Glass, Inc.™, Armaflex®, Axor®, BainUltra® Meridian™, Band-Aid®, Basco®, Basco AquaGlide®, Bedrock®, Bemis® Purité™, Benjamin Moore®, Bostik®, Broan®, Brondell™ Swash™, California, Faucets®, Caroma®, Century Bathworks®, C.H. Hanson®, Chicago Faucets®, Chloraloy®, Cold Shield™, Continental Fan™, Corian®, Daltile®, Danze®, Delta®, Delta® Leland®, DensArmor®, DensShield®, DitraSet™, Dow Corning®, Dupont®, Duravit®, Durock®, EarthSource Forest Products®, EasyHeat®, Eljer®, ENERGY STAR®, Enviroglas®, Fantech®, Festool® Domino®, FibaFuse®, Finlandia Sauna®, Flor®, Fortiber's Aquabar®, Gerber®, Gerberit®, Georgia-Pacific®, GreenGlass®, Grohe®, Hakatai®, Hampton®, Hansgrohe®, Hansgrohe Axor®, HardieBacker®, Home Ventilating Institute®, Hot Stop®, Hy-Lite®, Infloor®, James Hardie®, Kohler® Memoirs®, Kohler Devonshire®, Kohler Persuade®, Kohler Purist Hatbox®, Kohler Stillness®, Kohler Symbol™, Kohler WaterTile™, Kohler®, Lacava®, Leviton®, Liberty Pumps®, Lowe's®, Lutron®, Mansfield® EcoQuantum™, Marktime®, Moen®, MoistureShield™, Motiv®, MTI Whirlpools®, Niagara Conservation®, Noble Company®, NobleSeal®, NobleFlex®, NuHeat™, NuTone®, Oceanside Glasstile®, Panasonic®, Pittsburgh Corning™, Porcher Époque®, Price Pfister® Catalina®, Profin™, ProSpec®American, Protecto Wrap®, Quikrete®, Rain-X®, Rehau®, Rejuvenation®, Rockler®, Romex®, Saniflo®, Satin Impervo®, Schlüter®-Kerdi®, SeaTech Inc.®, Sears®, Silestone®, Solatube®, St. Thomas Creations®, Standard Ceramix®, STEP Warmfloor™, Sterling®, Sun Tunnel™, SunTouch®, SunTouch® LoudMouth™, Super Glue™, Symbol™, Symmons®, Tamarack Airetrak®, Teflon®, The Home Depot®, The Standard Collection®, TimberStrand®, Toto Aquia®, Toto Clayton®, Toto Neorest®, Toto®, Uponor®, Velux®, Velux Sun Tunnel®, VentZone Systems®, Viessmann®, Villeroy & Boch®, Vortens™, WaterSense®, WaterTile™, WattsRadiant™, Watts®, WhisperCeiling™, WhisperGreen®, Whitehaus®, Zurn®

About Your Safety: Homebuilding is inherently dangerous. From accidents with power tools to falls from ladders, scaffolds, and roofs, builders risk serious injury and even death. We try to promote safe work habits through our articles. But what is safe for one person under certain circumstances may not be safe for you under different circumstances. So don't try anything you learn about here (or elsewhere) unless you're certain that it is safe for you. Please be careful.

Except for new page numbers that reflect the organization of this collection, these articles appear just as they did when they were originally published. You may find that some information about manufacturers or products is no longer up to date. Similarly, building methods change and building codes vary by region and are constantly evolving, so please check with your local building department.

Special thanks to the authors, editors, art directors,

copy editors, and other staff members of *Fine Homebuilding*

who contributed to the development of the articles in this book.

CONTENTS

PART 2: PLUMBING AND HARDWARE

PART 3: BATHROOM FLOORS AND WALLS

PART 4: LIGHTING, HEATING, VENTILATION

INTRODUCTION

For only a few dollars per square foot, you can upgrade from an ordinary fiberglass shower to a ceramic-tiled shower surround. The inexpensive tiled shower will require more maintenance than the fiberglass and may look only marginally better. But if you can afford to kick in a few extra dollars to add a band of glass or a handful of accent tiles to the surround, you can quickly start to make the project sing. Of course, if you're not careful with your budget, you can easily blow your retirement on tile, too.

If you are reading this book, you are likely going to be starting a bathroom remodel soon. You can use the book as a reference during your project. The information here comes from *Fine Homebuilding* magazine, which is known for publishing the best how-to information available.

Making the most of a small space requires thoughtful planning. To avoid mistakes, it's a good idea to work out all the details before you settle on any materials or run any plumbing. Your budget is important, but there are some decisions that transcend cost. Consider the finish on a faucet, for instance. In a high-use bathroom, the durability provided by a more expensive PVD finish is worth the upcharge. A faucet with this space-age technology is also likely to have higher-quality components inside. Likewise, water-conserving fixtures may cost more money up front but will result in savings down the road.

While the old saying "you get what you pay for" is definitely true in bathroom material, there are plenty of smart ways to save money, too. You'll find lots of ideas to make up for your necessary splurges in the first chapter of this book. Bathroom remodeling is hard work, which brings one more old saying to mind, "do it right, do it once."

—Brian Pontolilo, editor
Fine Homebuilding

Bathroom Remodeling on Any Budget

■ BY PAUL DeGROOT

If you live in an older home, I bet you have at least one bathroom that you dislike. Maybe the floors or fixtures are worn out, maybe the bath is cramped and lacks storage space, or maybe too many people share it. Regardless of the problems, one thing is always true: You need to make informed design decisions and smart material choices to remodel a bath successfully. My projects typically fall into three categories: makeovers, expansions, and additions. Occasionally, they involve elements of more than one approach (see p. 16 for examples). Choosing what is right for you means balancing construction costs (see the sidebar on pp. 6–7) with your desired result. Once you have a plan in hand, you'll have to make a lot of decisions about materials. Here's the best advice I can offer.

Start with the Big Three: Sink, Toilet, and Tub

Enameled cast iron and porcelain dominated the fixture market in my grandparents' day. Sinks, toilets, and tubs made from these materials were durable and affordable. Those qualities are still essential today, along with water conservation, safety, comfort, and style.

Countertop-mounted sinks include undermounts that attach below the surface for easy cleanup. While these sinks aren't necessarily pricey, installation can be. Most undermount sinks require expensive slab counters such as stone or quartz. They also require that the hole be cut perfectly, with the edges polished smooth. A drop-in or self-rimming sink is less fussy to install, and the counter can be laminate or another affordable material. Consider a pedestal or wall-mounted sink when space is limited but a counter and vanity storage aren't necessary.

Sink color and shape are design choices that don't affect performance. Check the depth of the vanity cabinet, though: 21-in.-deep bath cabinets are common, and some larger sinks require a 24-in. cabinet.

Flushing efficiency and comfort are the critical factors when it comes to toilets. Water-conservation concerns have forced manufacturers to design toilets that are more adept at flushing. Some are better than others, so read the reviews before buying. You can find a good two-piece toilet for $200 or less. One-piece models, which are easier to clean, cost more. Roomier seats are generally found on toilets with elongated bowls. Taller folks might find a higher toilet more comfortable.

Tubs with jets and other therapeutic features have electric motors mounted below the platform, and access is required for service. If you are considering a jetted tub, read the manual first to ensure your bathroom meets the electrical, structural, and spatial requirements. Also, be sure that your water

A Makeover

A makeover is generally easier and less expensive than the other project categories. No walls are moved, and plumbing, windows, and doors are left in place. The most common targets to upgrade are floors, fixtures, lights, fans, and countertops. Updating cabinetry may entail only fresh paint or new drawer fronts and doors. Controlling material costs is a matter of making smart decisions and using expensive materials where they matter most. It's important to note, however, that construction costs can still get out of control in a makeover project if you don't consider everything carefully. For example, swapping a vanity for a pedestal sink may mean replacing the floor as well.

An Expansion

If a bathroom is well located within the floor plan of the house but is too small or lacks the features you want, you'll need to plan for an expansion. A bathroom on an outside wall can be bumped outward. But a bump-out needs a foundation, a roof, and exterior walls, which are more expensive than allocating space within the footprint. If you can commandeer 6 sq. ft. from an adjacent room or closet, you'll have enough space to add a second sink or a linen closet to your bath, and construction costs will not be nearly as expensive as an addition.

An Addition

There are situations when building an entirely new bathroom is necessary. A typical starter home has only two bedrooms and one bath. Add children to the family, and the household soon needs an additional bathroom. This is often the right time to add a master suite, and use the original two bedrooms and bath for the kids and guests. It's an expensive project, but the alternative—a bigger house—is not only more expensive but also means moving.

All bath additions have this in common: costs associated with connecting to the existing sewer line. Tying a new drain line into an existing one is always less expensive than running a new dedicated sewer line to the street or basement. This is especially true for an upstairs addition; getting a new sewer line down through the lower floors can be tricky. Talk to your plumber about it early in the process.

heater can supply enough hot water to fill the tub.

Soaking tubs come in many shapes, lengths, and depths. The ubiquitous 60-in.-long tub is about 14 in. tall and holds a 10-in. depth of water. That's fine for kids, and the tub is safe to step in and out of when used for a shower. If you want more of your body submerged when bathing, however, choose a taller tub.

Porcelain-enameled cast-iron tubs are expensive, but can last a lifetime. Due to the weight and cost of cast iron, however, many new tubs are made of lighter materials. Most jetted-tub makers use acrylic or gel-coated fiberglass. The finish on acrylic is generally thicker and more durable than the gel coat. Some soaking tubs are made from light-gauge pressed steel with a porcelain finish. Be wary of thin-walled tubs, especially if you plan to tile the surround. If the tub finish scratches, cracks, oxidizes, or fades, you'll need to tear out the tile to upgrade.

Price: Low (Makeover)
No walls were harmed in this guest-bathroom makeover, but the room was completely gutted, and all new fixtures, cabinets, finishes, and accessories were installed.

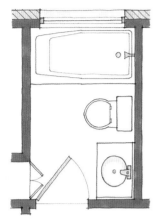

BEFORE

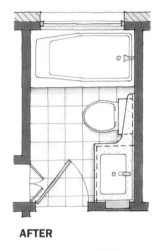

AFTER

0   1   2   4 ft.

BALANCING THE BUDGET

Staying within the existing
footprint and reusing the
existing window, door, and
light fixture kept money in the
budget for a glass-tile accent
wall; Italian porcelain floor
and wall tile; custom white-oak
cabinets, mirror frame, and wall
niche; Silestone® countertop
and backsplash; undermount
sink; and Grohe® faucet.

Tile Rules for Bathroom Floors

Ceramic tile is hard to beat for bath floors.
It's affordable and easy to clean, and tiling is
something a patient homeowner can tackle.
So what's the downside? The biggie is that
a tile floor is only as good as the substrate
below it. Before installing tile, you should
strengthen the floor joists if they deflect;
replace rotten, missing, or bouncy subfloor-
ing; and if you're working on a slab, make
sure it's not cracked.

When choosing tile for a bathroom,
porcelain is the best because it's impervious
to moisture. Avoid glazed tiles that will be
slippery when wet. Look for a coefficient
of friction (COF) rating of 0.5 or higher to
ensure that the tile will not be a slip hazard.
Although small glass tiles are stylish and
waterproof, they expose more grout than
larger tiles, and grout is not impervious to
water unless diligently sealed.

Stone tile is also durable enough to make
a great bathroom floor. But if the floor will
get wet, a polished finish is no good. Honed
or flamed granite, matte travertine, and
most slate provide a natural grip. All stone
should be sealed, and some soft, porous
stones like marble will need frequent reseal-
ing to keep up their prized appearance. Of
course, most stone is more expensive to
purchase than ceramic tile and may dictate a
more expensive mortar-bed installation.

For a slab-on-grade bath, consider stained
concrete as an economical flooring option.
Sheets of glue-down linoleum, cork, and
vinyl flooring are also possibilities, but I
would not recommend the tile versions of
these materials. In each of these categories,
the better-looking products are still moder-
ate in price. Wood flooring in all bathrooms
should be avoided; one overflow is all it
takes to ruin it.

Price: Moderate (Expansion)

This project is primarily a master-bath makeover, with 5 sq. ft. stolen from two adjacent hall closets, which allowed the toilet and the vanity to be relocated. The corner shower stayed in place but was expanded to a more comfortable size.

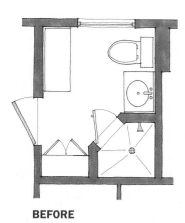

BEFORE

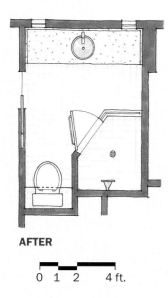

AFTER

0 1 2   4 ft.

BALANCING THE BUDGET

Saving on painted flat-panel
cabinets and white ceramic floor
and wall tile, as well as minimiz-
ing the amount of plumbing work,
freed up money for a vessel sink,
an Enviroglas® countertop and
backsplash, aqua-colored glass
mosaic wall tile, and the construction costs of expanding into the
closets. The expansion alternative—bumping out into the backyard—would have cost much more
in labor and materials.

Wet Walls Should Stay Dry

Besides being suitable for bathroom floors,
tile is also the answer for durable, attractive
shower walls. The only maintenance needed
is sealing and occasional regrouting. Small
grout joints tend to stay clean longer than
wide joints simply because there's less surface area. If you want small grout joints,
choose large machine-made tiles. With their
perfectly straight, "rectified" edges, such tiles
are uniform from one to the next. Handmade,
antique, and tumbled tiles require wider
joints. One way to get waterproof, mold-
proof joints is to use epoxy grout. Because
epoxy grout is expensive, smelly, and challenging to work with, hire a professional.

Glass tiles and stones that are dense
enough to polish, such as granite, travertine,
and marble, make attractive shower walls
that shed water and are easy to clean. Glass
tiles are expensive, though, so I often limit
them to where they make the biggest impact.

Acrylic and fiberglass tub and shower surrounds may be the most affordable option
for shower walls. Although they are not very
stylish, they can look new for a long time.

One final choice to consider is glass
block, which looks good, cleans up well, and
lets light filter into the shower. If anything,
the sanded grout will be what shows grime
and mildew over time, so consider using
silicone grout. If you think glass block is
expensive, remember that it is the entire
wall. Compared with the combined cost of
studs, sheathing, backerboard, and tile, glass
block may not be that costly after all.

Price: High (Addition)

With limited and clumsy closets, the original master bath had nowhere to grow. It was tiny and landlocked. Tearing it out made space for a new walk-in closet. Busting into the side yard with the master-bath addition yielded three exterior walls for abundant daylight and preserved backyard views from the bedroom.

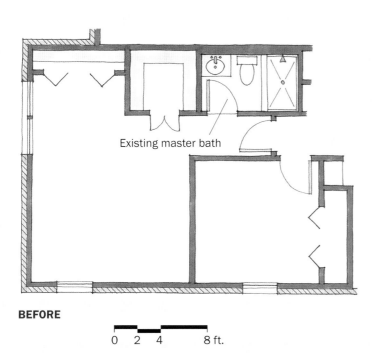

Existing master bath

BEFORE

0　2　4　　　8 ft.

BALANCING THE BUDGET

Savings were few on this project, but the homeowners decided that they could do without a tub, which did save space for an oversize doorless shower. The splurges that make this bath so special include clerestory windows, sapele-veneered cabinets, Italian porcelain floor and wall tile, glass mosaic shower tile, a Silestone countertop, undermount sinks, Grohe faucets, and a comfort-height Toto® toilet. Hey, not everyone needs to save.

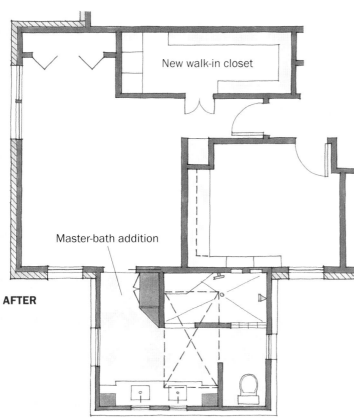

New walk-in closet

Master-bath addition

AFTER

The Powder-Room Premium

I think powder rooms are great opportunities to include splashes of premium materials that tell friends, family, and visitors that they're worth it. Like your front door, your public privy sends an impression about what kind of ship you run. Upgrading the floor tile from utilitarian to übercool won't empty your wallet because the floor just isn't that big. Switching from a painted vanity to one made of cherry or walnut might add only a few hundred dollars because it's a petite cabinet to start with. Likewise, a fancy mirror or faucet might be only $100 more than a plain one.

Borrowing an idea from a friend's powder room, my neighbor wanted to have some fun with the mirror above her pedestal sink. So we recessed plain mirror glass into a niche in the wall and lined the opening with mosaic tile in a vibrant red (photo at right). It's a real eye-catcher as you come in the door, and the little shelf is perfect for decorative accessories.

For an accent wall in the powder room at our house, I ran the 12-in. limestone floor tile up the wall behind the toilet. At $5 per tile, it didn't cost much, and it's a lovely contrast to the rich paint color my wife chose for the other walls. I added a small mahogany trim strip up high around the room, sort of a modern version of the traditional picture molding and an inexpensive but beautiful detail. The little mahogany picture shelf that I mounted above the toilet is simple and elegant (top photo facing page). Finally, because I was building it myself, I did something a little different with the cabinet doors to add interest (bottom photo facing page).

Glass Shower Doors Let in the Light

Most bathtubs get little use. If space is limited, consider nixing the tub for a slightly bigger shower. A 3½-ft. by 5-ft. shower is much more comfortable than a 3-ft. by 3-ft. postage stamp and leaves room for a seat.

Nearly all stand-alone showers have glass doors to keep in water, steam, and heat (for more on shower doors, see p. 77). Glass makes a small shower feel bigger and allows light to invade. Doors and panels surrounded by aluminum frames are less costly than frameless assemblies. The aluminum extrusions surrounding the glass give it strength, so the glass can be thinner. Some homeowners choose to maximize the glass area by using more expensive frameless enclosures. Showers designed so that no door is necessary require a slightly bigger footprint, but make for an open-feeling bath.

Don't Buy Cheap Cabinets

Replacing a worn-out vanity and countertop is an effective makeover project. Spend your money wisely, and this simple upgrade can last decades. The best advice is this: Don't cut costs. You may need only one cabinet (and a small countertop), but it's going to live in a moisture-rich environment where particleboard cases and cheap hardware won't last long.

Light the Mirror, and Ventilate Well

Recessed lights are affordable, but because they send most of their light downward in a cone-shaped pattern, they're not the best choice for a small room. Still, codes prohibit exposed bulbs near a shower, so recessed lights with glass diffusers are one of the only options. Budget-level plastic diffusers are cheap, and they turn yellow. The use of

1: AN ARTFUL ADDITION

Price: Moderate-High (Addition)

Pushing out the walls of this house made sense because the homeowners were looking for more than a new bathroom. They wanted an art studio, too. Although the new master bath remains within the original footprint, the addition made it possible.

BEFORE

0 2 4   8 ft.

AFTER

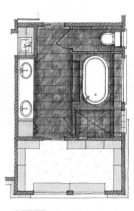

BALANCING THE BUDGET

There were some savings on bath fixtures (like the base-model exhaust fans and inexpensive lighting), but it was combining the bath remodel with a larger project that allowed these homeowners to splurge on a deep cast-iron Kohler® soaking tub, bisque-colored Kohler cast-iron sinks, frameless shower glass, an onyx countertop, and slate floor and wall tile.

compact-fluorescent bulbs may delay yellowing and save you money.

Surface-mounted lights are the work-horses of vanity lighting. If your design or budget dictates but one light, put it above the mirror, and pick a fixture that sends light up, down, and outward. If there's enough wall area and enough money in the budget, flank the mirror with two surface-mounted fixtures.

Most bathroom fans are recessed into the ceiling and are ducted outside the house.

2: FOUND SPACE FOR A NEW GIRLS' BATH

Price: Moderate (All New)

This family gave up a game room for new bedrooms and a bathroom for their three young girls. Rearranging walls within the existing footprint was an affordable way to get what they needed without adding square footage or the cost of an addition.

0   2   4   8 ft.

BALANCING THE BUDGET

The most significant costs in this project involved the demolition and construction of interior walls and the installation of new plumbing runs. Saving on materials, such as painted cabinets, drop-in sinks, and inexpensive tile for the counter and floor left money in the budget for a built-in dresser.

Inexpensive bathroom-fan models tend to be loud, so shop for a fan that has a sone rating of less than 1.0 if peace and quiet are important considerations for you. Vent-fan manufacturers offer many combinations of lighting, exhaust, and supplemental room heating with their models. These fixtures can be more affordable than purchasing and installing each feature separately.

Architect Paul DeGroot (www.degrootarchitect.com) *designs custom homes and additions in Austin, Texas.*

3: ONE SINK TOO MANY

BALANCING THE BUDGET
Affordable paint-grade cabinetry, a drop-in sink, and ceramic counter, floor, and wall tiles left enough money in the budget for a new window, the removal of a wall, and plumbing modifications that allowed tub and toilet to be relocated.

Price: Low (Makeover)

A wall within the bathroom separated the tub and toilet area from the double sinks in this small hall bath that was remodeled for a young boy. Taking down the wall and removing a sink made room for a linen closet and for turning the tub 90°. The result is a more spacious-feeling room within the existing footprint.

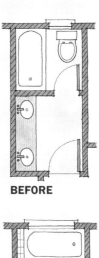

BEFORE

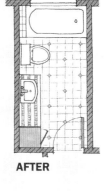

AFTER

0   2   4   8 ft.

The Perfect Master Bath

■ BY STEPHEN VANZE

We've all seen them. They appear in magazines at the checkout line and the convenience-store counter, just above the reach of small children. The pictorial spreads, full of glossy color photos, make you ache with desire. We see them at friends' houses (at least the friends we know well enough to let us see them). Some of our friends even carry pictures of them in their wallets.

What are they? I'm talking about big, beautiful master bathrooms with marble floors, marble counters, gold-plated sinks and faucets, showers that produce water from every direction, and floors that are slightly warm to the touch. These baths have features that you never knew existed but now you cannot live without. They make you contemplate a home-equity loan and conferences with architects and builders.

Here's a reality check: These showcases can become very big and very expensive.

Sculptural elements distinguish a bath. In a house with Craftsman-style detailing, this custom double-bowl lavatory with matching mirrors echoes similar elements in adjacent rooms.

*The next time
you're looking at
a picture of the
bathroom you've
always wanted,
try figuring out
how big that
bathroom is.*

The relationship of master bedroom, dressing area, bathroom, and entry into the suite from the hallway should be the foremost planning principle.

Start by Analyzing the Space

The next time you're looking at a picture of the bathroom you've always wanted, try figuring out how big that bathroom is. A typical tub deck is at least 3½ ft. wide and almost 7 ft. long. A two-sink counter is almost certainly 6 ft. long and 2 ft. deep. The shower is probably 4 ft. square, and the space in the middle of the room, with the chair and the small dressing table, is around 5 ft. wide and 8 ft. long.

The bathroom on p. 19 is 11 ft. by 17 ft. To get a sense of how big this space is, start measuring some other rooms in your house. This dream bathroom likely will be the biggest room in your house. It is probably bigger than most of your bedrooms, a bit narrower than your dining room, and about the size of your eat-in kitchen.

Now do a quick check on the cost of fixtures and materials. Check the price of a cast-iron whirlpool tub (about $3,000) and the incredibly beautiful sink faucet you see in that magazine picture (easily $900). These costs are on top of the marble that ranges from $70 to $80 per sq. ft. or molded tiles that cost $25 each. A luxuriously appointed large master bathroom, built in an existing space, will end up costing $25,000 to $40,000 as well as taking up about one third of your second floor. For this price tag, you could have several fairly nice vacations in hotels with bathrooms that sexy.

Of course, there's the other extreme: the practical, minimally sized bathroom that has everything you need but nothing you want. This room might be the master bathroom you have now: one sink and a tub/shower combination with the toilet next to it.

HALLWAY CENTERED
The door between the master bedroom and the master bath is usually open. Therein lies opportunity. Centering the hallway can focus the view on attractive elements in each room.

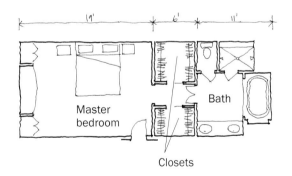

Closets

HALLWAY TO THE SIDE
If the entry to the master suite passes by the bathroom, the designer has a different sort of opportunity: Create a pair of discrete dressing rooms separate from the bedroom.

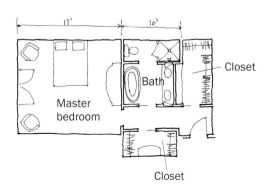

Closet

Create a space for each function. You can give the bath a roomlike feel by organizing its functions around a central space. Here, the tub alcove and the recessed lavatory counter show two ways to apply this rule.

In a small bath, fixtures take on great prominence. A cast-iron tub with faceted corners surrounded by tumbled marble tile distinguishes this bath.

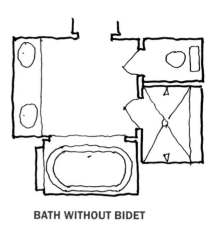

Try to control growth. If the bathroom has to grow to accommodate function, keep it to a minimum. For example, in these two central-square plans, adding a bidet to the water closet steals a bit of space from the shower.

BATH WITHOUT BIDET

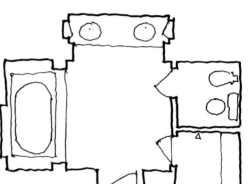

BATH WITH BIDET

The room is only 8 ft. square, has inexpensive but functional fixtures and 4×4 tile, and serves its purpose to the bare minimum. But in that room, you don't want to lounge and enjoy getting ready in the morning. And you're certainly not going to show it to your friends.

So how do you strike a balance? Where is the middle ground that satisfies your need to be pampered but doesn't involve the creation of the bathroom that ate your bank account and your house?

First, you need to remember the essential functions and elements of a master bathroom. They are washing, bathing, and using the toilet. But instead of fulfilling just these obvious and minimal requirements, the master bathroom can be an extension of your personal living quarters, part of your bedroom.

The master suite includes a sleeping area, a dressing area, and the bath. The master bathroom is a place where you can perform your daily toilette in a pleasant environment that allows you and, if attached, your significant other to enjoy preparing for the day ahead or to relax while getting ready for bed. In much the same way that the kitchen has become more than just a room to prepare meals and more of a place where the whole family can gather, the master bath has become more than just a bathroom in recent years. How do you make this room a pleasant place to start the day without breaking the bank? I have six suggestions that can help you plan that perfect bath.

Make your bathroom a room. Don't line the fixtures against a wall.

Six Design Tips

1. THE BATH AND THE BEDROOM NEED A COMFORTABLE CONNECTION

Consider the bathroom in the context of your entire master suite and bedroom floor. The relationship of master bedroom, dressing area, bathroom, and entry into the suite from the hallway should be the foremost planning principle. Hire an architect or another design professional to help you. On p. 20 are two generic plans of master-bedroom suites. The first shows a bedroom entered from the hall; from the bedroom, you pass through a dressing area into the master bath. The bathroom is the farthest space from the entry and is therefore the most private (see the top drawing on p. 20).

The second plan shows the entrance to the master suite via a dressing room, with a bathroom off a vestibule-like space (see the bottom drawing on p. 20). While making the bathroom less private, it allows for one half of a couple to get up, get washed, get dressed, and leave without bothering his or her lucky, still-sleeping partner.

In both schemes, the bathrooms are not the biggest spaces; the bedrooms are. The bathrooms are big enough, but not too big compared with the other spaces. Both bathrooms are adequate and comfortable without being opulent.

2. DESIGNATE SPACES FOR SPECIFIC FUNCTIONS

Design a specific space for each of the most essential functions. For washing, design a contained counter area (see the photo on p. 19) or a wall against which a sculptural pedestal sink can be displayed. The same holds true for the tub, shower, and toilet area. Decide if you really need a separate tub and shower or if a combined shower/tub, or even just a shower, will serve your purposes. Determine if the toilet needs its own room or whether it can be part of the open bathroom. Where fixtures are more artistic, keep some wall space clear so that they can shine.

A toilet with its own room requires more space. If space is limited, incorporating a well-designed toilet as a beautiful element in the bathroom itself can help to make the bath seem bigger and airier.

3. MAKE YOUR BATHROOM A ROOM

Don't line the fixtures against a wall. Instead, organize different functional areas around a central space, and give this space a roomlike feel (see the photo on p. 21). Decide on the minimum space you need to move around in, and try not to let that grow. On p. 23 are two floor plans where each function is in its own space, with each organized around a central square.

4. THE BATH SHOULD BE AN EXTENSION OF THE BEDROOM

When the bathroom door is open, which it usually is, what do you see from the bedroom? Do you look at a beautiful tub in an arched alcove with a small window facing your thoughtfully manicured backyard? Or do you see a toilet with the seat up? Conversely, carefully consider what you see from the bathroom (see the photo on p. 20). While lying in the tub enjoying a good soak, is your main focus the hamper full of dirty clothes, or is it across the bedroom out the window? Use the bathroom to make the bedroom bigger and vice versa.

5. USE COMPATIBLE FIXTURES AND MATERIALS

Carefully select fixtures and materials in keeping with your tastes and with the essential character of your home. If you live in a 1920s bungalow, stick with a tile that reflects that period, or use tongue-and-groove beadboard that picks up other features of the house. But don't make the bathroom the most nicely appointed room in the house. Although it is a place where you spend a lot of time, you entertain there only infrequently. Hire a designer sympathetic to your tastes and to your home. Don't believe expensive means better. Many beautiful, inexpensive light

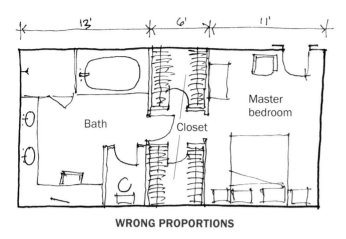

WRONG PROPORTIONS

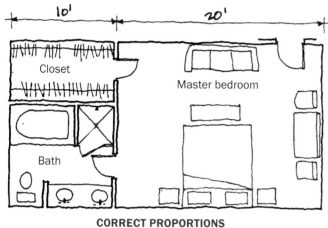

CORRECT PROPORTIONS

DON'T LET THE BATH TAKE OVER THE BEDROOM
Maintain balance in a master suite by keeping the bathroom smaller than the bedroom. Although the bath should be a pleasant space to be in, it shouldn't put the rest of the house to shame.

fixtures, faucets, and plumbing fixtures can be used in lieu of the most expensive.

If you fall in love with a particular fixture outside your price range, ask yourself why you like it. Once you identify the attractive qualities, you can take them to a design professional who can help you to find a similar fixture within your price range.

6. KEEP IT IN PROPER PROPORTION

Always consider that your design response is proportional to the problem. If you have decided that your tub is a little too small, don't take away from the master bedroom to make the tub bigger. When you are done planning, look over your bathroom plan. It should be smaller than your bedroom and, ideally, smaller than your dining room. Although you should enjoy being in the bath, it should not be the place where you stay all day because the rest of the house is so depressing by comparison. Study the drawings above for the correct proportions for a 15-ft. by 30-ft. master suite.

If you follow these steps, you will have a master bathroom that reflects your style, that enhances your house, and that gives you one more reason to get up in the morning.

Stephen Vanze is a principal in the firm Barnes Vanze in Washington, D.C.

When you are done planning, look over your bathroom plan. It should be smaller than your bedroom and, ideally, smaller than your dining room.

Two Approaches to the Basement Bath

■ BY CHARLES MILLER

Minneapolis remodeler Greg Schmidt gets more and more calls these days for basement and attic remodels. Rather than build a new house, homeowners are looking to take advantage of the spaces they already have under their roof.

1. A Bath for a Basement Apartment

Last year, one of Schmidt's clients asked him to evaluate her 1,100-sq.-ft. basement to see if it could be converted into an apartment for her retired father. Schmidt was impressed by the generous 8-ft. ceilings in the basement, and by the size of the seven windows scattered throughout. It would make a terrific apartment.

Central to the goal of making the space into a home was creating a comfortable bathroom full of architectural details similar to those found elsewhere in the house.

DECIDING WHERE THE BATH SHOULD GO WAS THE EASY PART

Part of the basement makeover needed to include a relocated laundry area, and during the initial site visit, Schmidt realized only one place would work: between the laundry chute and the existing drain lines. The bathroom logically shared this proximity to plumbing, which included the main soil stack draining the entire house. The stack was right in the middle of what would become the new bath.

Don't forget the cleanout. Held in place by screws nesting in trim washers, a removable panel at the column base leads to the soil-stack cleanout.

A subtle geometry lesson. The oval shape of the lavatory is repeated in the glass shelf below and the mirror above, establishing an underlying unity to the decor. The subway wall tiles and hexagonal floor tiles repeat details from the upstairs baths.

Constraints can be your friend. Moving the drain line would have been a major hassle. Rather than reroute it, builder Greg Schmidt wrapped it with frame-and-panel trim, transforming it into an elegant column anchoring the half-wall that separates the toilet alcove from the lavatory. Blocks screwed to the wall and epoxied to the drain line anchor the column.

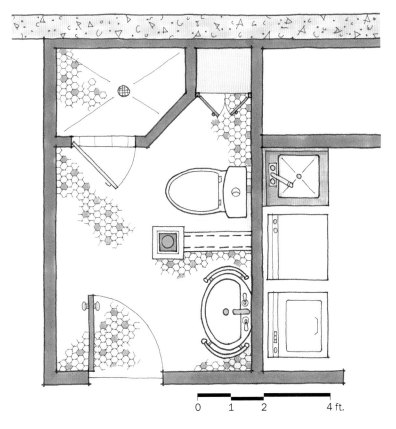

0   1   2   4 ft.

Sources

Console table and lavatory:
The Standard Collection® by American Standard®

Mirror with medicine cabinet:
The Standard Collection by American Standard

Hampton® widespread faucet:
The Standard Collection by American Standard

Toilet: Toto colonial white Dalton

Rather than move the stack, Schmidt turned it into an architectural focal point and an organizational element in the plan. As a Craftsman column (see the photo on p. 27 and the drawing on the facing page), the stack anchors a half-wall that separates the lavatory side of the bath from the toilet side.

Design and construction: Greg Schmidt (www. homerestorationinc.com), Minneapolis, Minnesota.

Builder's Notes: Column Details

The first thing people notice about this bathroom is the column trim. It had to mimic a structural column to look right. To that end, I split the column into three components: a lower, plinth-like base portion that wraps both the soil stack and the end of the half-wall, and a narrower upper portion that wraps the rest of the stack. A ledge atop the half-wall separates the two parts of the column and functions as a toiletry shelf. I wanted the base portion of the column to be strong enough to stand up to the errant shoe or vacuum nozzle.

As shown in the drawing, the base is a frame-and-panel assembly made of ³⁄₄-in. medium-density fiberboard (MDF) rails and stiles joined with loose tenons. I chose loose tenons for their extra strength, both in transit from shop to site and in place in the bath. I used my Festool® Domino® joiner (www.festoolusa.com) to cut the mortises for the tenons. Then I used my router to cut ¹⁄₂-in. by ¹⁄₂-in. rabbets on the back sides of the rails and stiles to accept glued-in-place ¹⁄₄-in. MDF panels.

The base is capped with a ³⁄₄-in.-thick MDF collar and a tail piece that serves as the shelf atop the half-wall. I assembled these on site and glued their loose tenons in place with gel-viscosity Super Glue™ speeded up with aerosol activator, both from Rockler® (www.rockler.com). I used a different, lighter-weight approach on the upper column. As shown in the detail, it is composed of ¹⁄₂-in. MDF, with ¹⁄₄-in.-thick MDF strips tacked and glued at the corners to mimic a frame-and-panel assembly. Like the lower column, its corners are softened with a ¹⁄₄-in.-radius router bit.

Mitered moldings dress up the columns' intersections and mimic the home's other trim details. After the components were on site, I finish-nailed

and glued them together. Then I filled the nail holes with joint compound and applied two coats of Benjamin Moore® Satin Impervo® over a coat of oil-based primer.

—*Greg Schmidt*

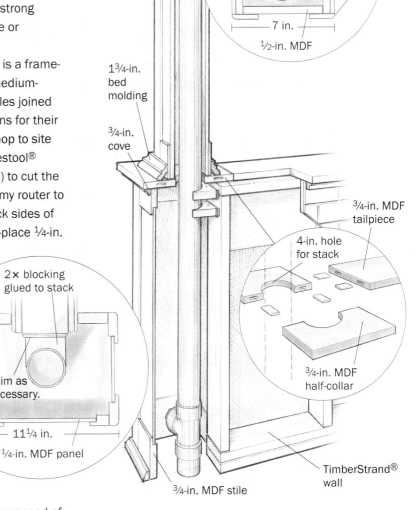

¹⁄₄-in. MDF overlay

3-in. ABS stack

¹⁄₄-in. radius

7 in.

¹⁄₂-in. MDF

1³⁄₄-in. bed molding

³⁄₄-in. cove

2× blocking glued to stack

¹⁄₂-in. rabbet

Shim as necessary.

11¹⁄₄ in.

¹⁄₄-in. MDF panel

³⁄₄-in. MDF tailpiece

4-in. hole for stack

³⁄₄-in. MDF half-collar

TimberStrand® wall

³⁄₄-in. MDF stile

Shower and steam room. In this basement spa, the family can stand beneath the showerheads or relax on a travertine bench and enjoy a steam bath. The heated towel bar helps keep the space free of excess moisture.

Full-scale blueprint. Marking the major elements of the bath with masking tape on the basement floor made it easier to evaluate how the plan would work. The shower space is at the top, the sauna to the left. A pocket door separates the two, an excellent application in this tight passageway.

2. A Spa Bath in the Basement

A couple with three young children acquired a house in Portland, Oregon, that included an 1,100-sq.-ft. unfinished basement. Thinking both short-term use and long-term utility, they hired designer/builder Paul Johnson to turn a portion of the basement into a multipurpose space that could be a playroom for the kids, a media room for the entire family, and a spare bedroom for overnight guests. In one corner, they carved out a spa bath that includes a steam shower big enough for the whole family, and a long-wished-for sauna.

TURNING AN OBSTACLE INTO AN ASSET

This is a family that likes to take steam baths together, and as such, they requested a bench in the shower big enough for everybody. Johnson had been thinking of the shower as a rectangular shape, but the corner where the shower needed to go had a jog in the foundation that limited the length of the bench. The longer he made the bench, the smaller the sauna got. The shower started to look like a hallway. And then, the obvious solution to the plan made itself apparent. Why not make two benches (see the photo on the facing page), one on each side of the foundation jog?

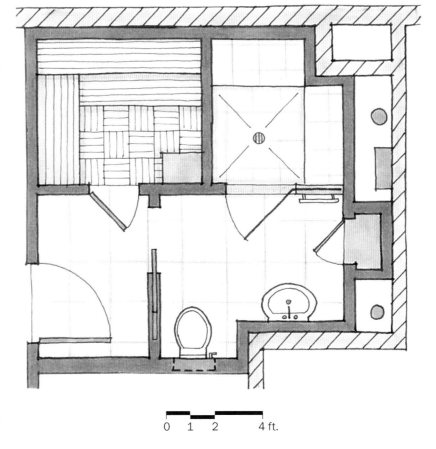

0   1   2   4 ft.

Minimizing Moisture Problems in a Basement Bath

The words *musty* and *basement* go together for good reason. Basement walls are cool, and moist air wants to condense on those cool surfaces, where it irrigates mold and leads to stale, musty odors. Adding a bathroom (typically without a window) to a basement can send the basement moisture meter sky high. Here's how these two baths deal with the problem.

IN BATH #1, A CLIMATE WITH EXTREME TEMPERATURE AND HUMIDITY SWINGS:

- **Closed-cell polyurethane** foam between the framing and the basement wall keeps the bathroom wall warm enough to minimize condensation.
- **Epoxy grout** prevents water penetration into the tile joints.
- **Large windows** in the rest of the basement and a 110-cfm bath fan promote airflow.
- **There's no AC,** but a dehumidifier helps when it gets sticky in the summer.
- **TimberStrand engineered studs** are used for straightness and stability in walls that have tile finishes.

IN BATH #2, A CLIMATE WITH LESS EXTREME TEMPERATURE AND HUMIDITY VARIATIONS:

- **A heated towel bar** and an electric radiant floor keep air temperatures and wall surfaces above the dew point.
- **A Panasonic® 110-cfm bath fan** on a 60-minute timer removes moisture.

Keep it simple, if possible. This wall-mounted toilet had just enough fall between the bowl and the sewer line to make a simple connection requiring no pumps. The cleanout cover, mounted in the baseboard, mimics the look of the flush buttons over the bowl.

With that decision made, the plan quickly fell into place. To get it across to his clients, Johnson took out blue masking tape and sketched in the spaces and fixtures at full scale (see the photo on p. 31).

WALL-MOUNTED TOILET SOLVES TWO PROBLEMS

Because the drain line is close to floor level in this part of the basement, a traditional floor-mounted toilet limited its placement in the plan. A wall-mounted toilet, on the other hand, could be installed where it worked best in the room. In addition, its in-wall tank frees up a couple of square feet of floor space, and lifting the bowl off the floor creates a sense of roominess, important in a small bath.

Design and construction: Paul Johnson (www. pauljohnsoncarpentry.com), Portland, Oregon.
Charles Miller *is special issues editor at* Fine Homebuilding.

Sources

Showerhead:
WaterTile™ by Kohler

Handheld shower:
Stillness® by Kohler

Pedestal sink:
Darling by Duravit®

Toilet:
Darling by Duravit

Faucet:
Symbol™ by Kohler

Wall sconces:
Sine by Motiv®

Sauna kit:
Finlandia Sauna®

Closet or Bath?

■ BY CHARLES MILLER

Charlie's bedroom was just about perfect. Upstairs in a Craftsman-era house designed a century ago by the great Bay Area architect Bernard Maybeck, the room overlooks a winding creek shaded by large oak trees. The only thing missing in Charlie's bedroom was the rest of the bathroom.

At the turn of the 20th century, it was common for a bedroom to have its own lavatory. Charlie's bedroom had this arrangement (see "Before" floor plan on p. 38); the bathing and toilet facilities were in a bathroom down the hall. As Charlie turned the corner into his teenage years, however, having his own full bath rose higher on the priority list. His bedroom closet was the logical piece of real estate for a bathroom expansion. But what about the lost storage? Replacing that was the other chess move.

A Signature Detail Restores Storage

Leslie Lamarre of TRG Architects in Burlingame, California, came up with a solution that simultaneously replaced the lost closet space and added a classic Craftsman detail to the room: a window seat flanked by cabinets.

The cabinets are 24 in. deep. That's enough for hanging clothes, and it's a more efficient use of space than the old 39-in.-deep closet. One cabinet has two rods for hanging shirts and pants. The other has shelves for clothes and a shoe rack on the inside of the door. Along with the generous drawers below bench level, the new storage space is a net gain over the original closet.

Window seat waiting to happen. The original bedroom (see the photo on the facing page) featured a generous window centered on the west wall and a doorway to a sink-only bath on the right. In the reconfigured bedroom, a pair of wardrobes frames the window. Drawer storage below is topped by a comfy window seat. Display space hovers above the scene. Photos taken at A on floor plan (p. 38).

Comfortable coexistence. The clean lines of modern fixtures and the room's restrained colors and textures are right at home with the broad window and door casings of the Craftsman-era house. Photo taken at B on floor plan (p. 38).

The cabinets are made of cherry but are stained with a brownish glaze to look like American elm, which is more in keeping with the West Coast Craftsman look. A cork floor and carpet squares from Flor® (see "Sources" on p. 39) round out the changes in the bedroom. Both materials have sustainable underpinnings. Plus, Flor carpets are designed to be recycled. The company even offers to pick up its carpets and to cart them away for recycling when it's time for replacement.

Long, Narrow, and Uncluttered

At a little more than 3 ft. wide and about 12 ft. long, Charlie's bath could have been a dark shooting gallery. Lamarre kept it light with sleek finishes, fixtures that hug the walls, and a glass shower door. Coke bottle green glass tile lines the shower and wraps the lower walls of the rest of the bath as wainscoting. Bands of variegated-glass

Emphasize the space. Horizontal bands of mosaic tile draw the eye toward the shower, where reflective glass tiles bounce the light around and wall-hugging showerheads intrude minimally on the space.

Filling in the Rest of the Bath

A closet that didn't use space efficiently gave way to a shower in the new bathroom.
Built-in cabinets flanking the bedroom window replaced the lost closet space, and then some.

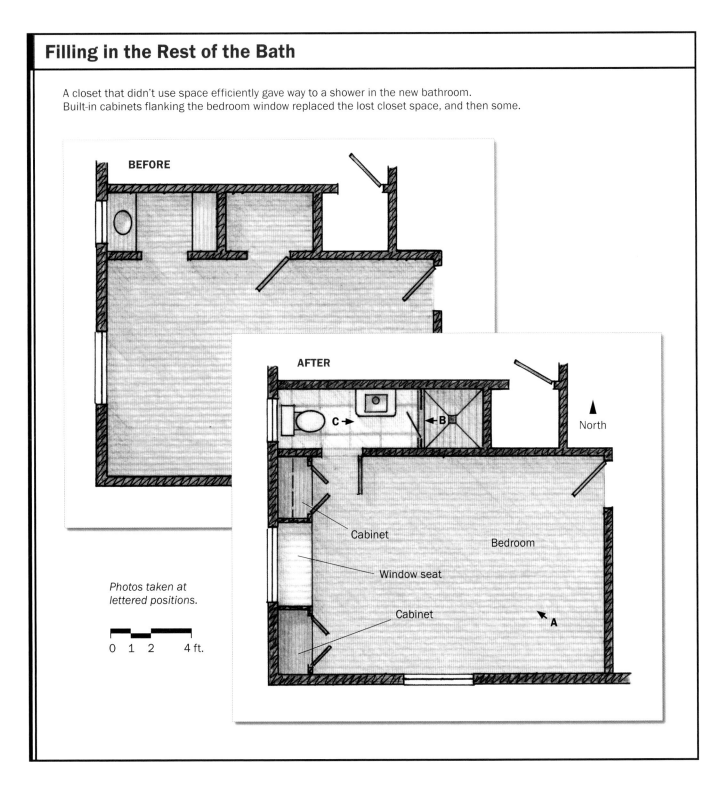

BEFORE

AFTER

North

Cabinet

Bedroom

Window seat

Cabinet

A

Photos taken at lettered positions.

0   1   2   4 ft.

mosaics tie it all together and emphasize the linear layout. A made-you-look detail of two silvery strips of aluminum runs like rails down the middle of the room, bordering the three rows of limestone floor tiles (see the left photo on the facing page).

A Lacava® wall-mounted sink, only 11 in. deep, doesn't crowd the room, yet it has enough deck space to rest a wet toothbrush and a bar of soap. Its chrome, T-shaped trap turns a typically unattractive collection of tubes into a sculptural detail. Even the

Aluminum strips in the floor add an edgy overtone. Photo taken at C on floor plan.

Sources

Body-spray showerheads:
www.kohler.com

Carpet:
www.flor.com

Glass tile:
Contemporanea Rainshower;
www.italics-stone.com

Lavatory:
Lacava Alia, AL026;
www.lacava.com

Shelf brackets:
www.expodesigninc.com

Toilet:
Toto, dual flush;
www.totousa.com

flush-mounted body-spray showerheads hug the walls, intruding as little as possible into the airspace.

The wall-mounted medicine cabinet originally specified in the plans (a unit with integral glass shelves) turned out to be way too expensive. As an alternative, a simple mirrored medicine cabinet is flanked by a set of three custom glass shelves supported by chrome wall brackets found online (see "Sources," above). They deliver the same look and utility for a lot less money. The shelves rise above the sink, providing space for items worthy of display, and they didn't add a lot to the budget.

Charles Miller is special-issues editor at Fine Homebuilding. *Builder: Charles Edward Inc.*

Two Baths from One

■ BY GENIE NOWICKI

I've worked as the designer on enough projects to know that remodeling is a fickle process. Nervous homeowners, discontinued products, and unforeseen construction obstacles are just some of the late-breaking curveballs thrown at a remodeling contractor. What happened on this job, though, was unique.

Midway through a major remodel of their home, the owners, who were happy with the plans and the progress so far, learned that they soon would have another child. The additional family member warranted an additional bathroom, and they wondered if I could work it into the plans.

I was willing to try, but it was going to be tricky. The homeowners had asked that the remodel not add any square footage to the house nor take away existing living space. They wanted to stick to that plan, and I wanted to honor their budget. Among their other requests were plenty of counter and storage space and natural light in each bathroom; a large shower in the master bath; a tub in the children's bathroom; and of course, beautiful finishes throughout.

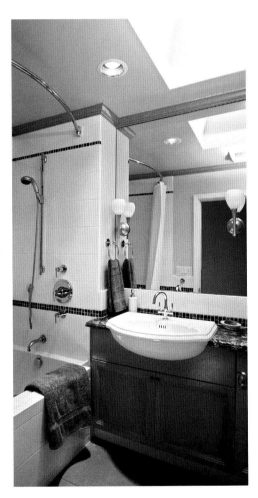

Kids' Bath

A small tub makes the most of this small bathroom. The curved hotel-style curtain rod creates a little extra elbow room for adults who use the shower. With a Hansgrohe® shower bar, the showerhead adjusts for bathers of all sizes. Photo taken at A on floor plan (see p. 42).

Master Bath

A creative arrangement squeezes the master bath into a small space. Recessed into the wall, the 6-in.-deep medicine cabinets don't crowd the shallow vanity. The Whitehaus® semirecessed full-size sinks maintain convenience stylishly. Photo taken at B on floor plan.

A Jog in the Wall, and Everything Fits

Before

Although the original bathroom was particularly large, about 127 sq. ft. (see the photo above), there was little room to spare when it was split in two. Dividing the space with a straight wall didn't work, but with a slight jog, a tub fit perfectly in the new kids' bathroom and left adequate clearance for the master-bath toilet. Squeezing the plumbing for three sinks, a toilet, and a tub/shower into one wall was another feat accomplished with detailed schematic drawings and good communication with the plumber.

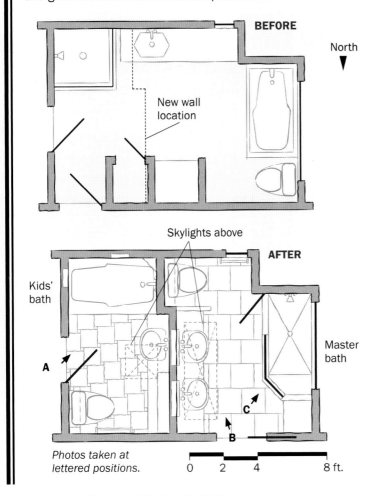

BEFORE

North ▼

New wall location

Skylights above

AFTER

Kids' bath

A

B

C

Master bath

Photos taken at lettered positions.

0   2   4   8 ft.

Shared Wall Optimizes Available Space

A bathroom with a standard shower-over-tub, a toilet, and a single-sink vanity requires at least 35 sq. ft. (a 5-ft. by 7-ft. room). Additional storage requires more space, and a typical master bath with two sinks, a tub, and a separate shower requires considerably more space.

Fortunately, one of the existing bathrooms was atypically large, about 127 sq. ft. (see the floor plan at left). If I wanted to get an additional bathroom into the house, I had to divide this space in two. To make the design work, I separated the master bath from the children's bathroom with a 2×6 wall. True, every inch counts, and a 2×4 wall would have saved floor space. But it would have been a tight fit for all the pipes required by the three sinks, the toilet, and the tub/shower that share the wall.

At a minimum, codes require 15 in. on each side of the centerline of a toilet and 24 in. clear in front of a toilet. A bit more space is much more comfortable. The toilet in the master bath was going to be a tight fit, so I created a jog in the plumbing wall with the toilet in the master bath on one side and the tub/shower in the kids' bathroom on the other. A 60-in.-long tub fit nicely between the walls in the children's bathroom, leaving 29 in. in front of the master-bath toilet. To provide plenty of elbow room for adults who might use the smaller shower in the kids' bath, I installed a curved, hotel-style shower-curtain rod (see the photo on p. 40).

Because the vanities share the interior wall, I was able to use the outside wall in the master bath for a sunlit walk-in shower. I angled the shower's outside corner to maintain a graceful entry into the room. The glass surround lends an open feel to the narrow space, a perception enhanced by custom-built cabinetry.

In the sunlit walk-in shower, you can choose the type of showerhead you like best. The glass surround creates an open feeling in the narrow bathroom. Photo taken at C on floor plan.

Shallow Cabinets Buy Floor Space

To maintain a reasonable amount of floor space in each bathroom without sacrificing storage, I designed shallow cabinets for the vanities and for the wall over each toilet. In the master bath, the vanity cabinets are only 12 in. deep; an 8-in.-deep cabinet fits in the wall recess above the toilet. Next to the shower is a full-height linen closet with a vented pull-out hamper at the base and roll-out shelves above. In the children's bathroom, the vanity cabinet is 15 in. deep and includes pull-out hampers. Shallow wall cabinets to the right of the sink and above the toilet provide more storage.

A Hybrid Skylight Brightens a Windowless Bath

To capture the open feeling of a splayed skylight well without the expense of installing a traditional skylight, a Velux® Sun Tunnel™ tubular skylight (www.veluxusa.com) was installed in a splayed well. The Sun Tunnel's flexible tube bends around existing roof framing to bring natural light into this interior bathroom. The tube terminates inside an 18-in.-deep by 30-in.-wide opening.

KIDS' BATH

Dome

Tubing

Diffuser

18 in.

30 in.

Two things make these shallow cabinets work: drawers with full-extension slides and semirecessed sinks. Most toiletries fit in small drawers; full-extension slides let you access even the smallest items that are pushed to the back of the drawer. Although the semirecessed sinks were a challenge for the stone-countertop fabricators, the design allows a full-size sink to be installed in a shallow vanity.

When space is limited, you can look to the wall cavity for help. I recessed the 6-in.-deep master-bath medicine cabinets into the stud bays of the wall so that they wouldn't overhang the narrow countertop. Because the kids' bath has plenty of storage, I was able to substitute a full-wall mirror for a medicine cabinet.

A Variety of Tiles Enhance the Countertop

Selecting bathroom finishes is a challenge for any homeowner. But again, this project presented a unique situation. The homeowners chose a single slab of green-and-black granite to be used for all the bathroom countertops. It was up to me to select tile that complemented the stone and gave each bathroom a distinct look and feel.

In the master bath, I used 12-in.-square Ming green, polished-marble tiles for the shower, with the same stone cut to 4-in.-square tiles for better traction on the shower floor. As an accent in the shower and at the vanity backsplash, I used black polished-granite tile in a running-bond (offset) pattern. This pattern repeats in the 16-in.-square matte-black slate tiles used on the floor. The backsplash and floor tiles not only complement the countertop granite but also highlight the rich cherry cabinetry.

In the kids' bathroom, I used 8-in. by 10-in. white ceramic tiles as a wainscot around the room and for the tub/shower surround. A band of 1-in.-square glass tiles in three different colors repeats the greens

and grays found in the countertop. The three colors were placed randomly to accentuate the room's playfulness. The floor is set in a pinwheel pattern, using 12-in.-square matte gray ceramic tiles and 2-in.-square black tumbled-marble inlays. With the light palette of tile and cabinetry, this interior bathroom stays bright and cheerful, particularly when sun shines through the skylight.

Skylights Wash the Rooms in Sunlight

Getting natural light into the master bathroom was no problem. We updated the two existing windows and modified the existing skylight to wash the room in sunlight. When night falls, recessed cans provide ambient lighting, and halogen sconces above the vanity soften shadows and provide task lighting.

Without exterior walls, bringing natural light into the children's bathroom was more challenging. Because of the intricate roof framing in the attic above, a traditional skylight was out of the question. The solution was a modified Sun Tunnel tubular skylight (see the sidebar on the facing page). Halogen sconce lights mounted on the mirror above the vanity and recessed can lights in the ceiling brighten the space even more.

Genie Nowicki is a certified kitchen, bath, and interior designer for Harrell Remodeling in Mountain View, California.

Better Roof, Better Bath

■ BY LISA CHRISTIE

Before

Jan and Tucker Mayberry's home has gone through a lot of changes since 1925. Originally a carriage house for a large estate, it was enlarged and reconfigured as a dwelling when the estate was sold. The bathroom ended up under a clumsy, flat-roofed dormer that poked through an otherwise lovely steep cedar roof. This bath housed a sink, a small dressing area, and a couple of closets. The toilet and shower were adjacent to the dormer in a dark space under a low roof.

The Mayberrys have been fixing up their house one space at a time, and that's given them time to decide exactly what they want the new spaces to be. General contractor Jay Lane, of Jack of the Woods Inc., has worked on numerous projects at their house over the past five years. When the time came to remodel the bathroom, Jay called my office. He knew our firm's experience would be a perfect fit.

The Mayberrys' goal for the bathroom was to make the most of its 10-ft. by 12-ft. size by bringing in more natural light, by adding another sink, by upgrading closet storage to accommodate two people, and by creating an attractive area for the toilet and

Part bath, part dressing room. The original bath didn't quite fit the style of the house . Now, furniture-grade vanities face one another, daylit by big windows overlooking the garden. The west wall is all closet space, and the travertine-tile floor is heated with an electric mat. Photos taken at B on floor plan (p. 49).

Small Change, Big Payoff

The new bathroom has the same layout as the old—toilet and shower in one area, sinks and closets in another—but two small improvements worked significant wonders. Widening the dormer by 4 ft. increased head height in the toilet/shower space, and adding another window brought in more natural light.

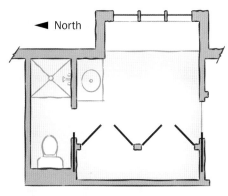

◄ North

BEFORE

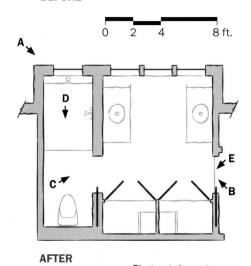

0   2   4   8 ft.

A

D

C

E

B

AFTER

Photos taken at lettered positions.

Curbless shower with a view.
Without the typical divider between the shower and the room, curbless showers make spaces seem larger. They are easier to clean and are safer than traditional showers because there is no curb to step over when the floor is wet and slippery. Photo taken at C on floor plan.

shower. The solution came by way of a new dormer and an opportunity to enhance the traditional architecture of the house.

Take the Roof to the Ridge

The new plan kept the original bathroom layout intact: toilet and shower in one area, sinks and closets in another (see the floor plans at left). Our decision to widen the dormer by 4 ft. and add a fourth window gained much-needed head height for the toilet/shower space, and flooded the bathroom with natural light. The new dormer has a much steeper roof, in keeping with the aesthetics of the house.

Next to the windows, two vanities face each other under a vaulted ceiling. The wall space above each sink is wide enough to accommodate large mirrors that conceal the medicine cabinets. Each one is flanked by wall-mounted sconces.

The other section of the new bath features a wall-mounted toilet by Duravit (www. duravit.com). Floor tile slides underneath the toilet with no interruption, making the area seem a bit larger; it's also easier to clean. The toilet tank is concealed in the wall. Typically, access to the tank is through a plastic panel mounted behind the toilet. However, such a panel didn't contribute to the traditional Craftsman feeling we were after. The contractor had an ingenious alternative: removable tiles (see "Great Idea" on p. 50)

Warmed by radiant-heat elements underneath, the floor is paved with tumbled travertine mosaics, balancing texture and scale with the larger wall tile.

Great Idea: Hidden Access Panel

By mounting three tiles on a piece of plywood, contractor Jay Lane created a removable access panel that blends in with the tile wainscoting behind the toilet. Metal clips on the back of the panel stick to a pair of magnets mounted to the wall framing. The magnets secured the panel while Jay "grouted" it in place with silicone caulk followed by a thin layer of the sanded grout used throughout the bath. You can't tell the panel apart from the rest of the wall; but if access to the toilet tank is ever needed, the sealant can be cut with a utility knife and the panel popped out without disturbing the rest of the tile. Photo taken at D on floor plan.

Bathroom Heaven, and the Stairway to It

With a new roof reaching to the ridge and more windows overlooking the garden, the revamped dormer looks as good outside as it does inside. However, the Mayberrys weren't excited about living through four months of dust, debris, and subcontractors tramping through their home. General contractor Jay Lane solved the problem by erecting scaffolding on the exterior for the duration of construction. All materials and workers entered and left the house straight through the front window-wall of the dormer. In addition, the scaffolding served as a great workspace and staging area. Photo taken at A on floor plan.

Mahogany and Travertine Set the Tone

Like other Craftsman homes of its era, this one has tile and stain-grade wood detailing throughout. We used similar materials in the bathroom but stepped it up a notch with tumbled travertine subway tile for the wainscoting; stone mosaics and tile chair-rail molding create a warm band of color at the top. The tile continues into the shower/ toilet space, where it nearly reaches the ceiling in the wet area.

The floor is tiled with tumbled travertine mosaics, balancing texture and scale with

A wall of closets. Behind bifold mahogany doors with full-length beveled-glass mirrors, the entire west wall of the bath is given over to storage. The combination of the new windows, the mirrored doors, and the vanity mirrors can make the whole room seem like it has windows everywhere. Photo taken at E on floor plan.

larger wall tile. The Mayberrys wake up to a warm floor courtesy of radiant-heating elements (www.nuheat.com) under the tile.

To re-create the look and feel of a traditional Craftsman room, we designed custom-made sink vanities, medicine cabinets, and closet doors of Honduras mahogany. Like furniture from the Craftsman era, the vanities have flush inset doors and drawers. Although less expensive, overlay doors and drawers just wouldn't look right in this context.

Lisa Christie is a principal at Christie Architecture LLC (www.Christiearchitecture.com) in Portland, Oregon.

The Seven Sins of Bathroom Design

■ BY PATRICK SUTTON

Bathrooms are botched more than any other room in the house. The big problem is water. It's central to the room's function, but it's a protean source of damage. And designers unduly focus on cosmetics at the expense of critically important construction basics.

Broadly speaking, the two causes of botched bathrooms are an unwillingness to spend the time and money it takes to construct a bathroom properly, and inept or inexperienced people handling the work. After 10 years of remodeling bathrooms, I've torn out a lot of other people's mistakes. Here is my list of the seven sins of bathroom design.

1. Inadequate Waterproofing

Bathrooms are wet rooms first, design showcases second. Every aspect of the planning and construction of bathrooms should take water exposure into account. If the waterproofing bill isn't at least 5 percent to 10 percent of the job cost, someone is cutting corners or doesn't know what she or he is doing. Badly made shower pans and improperly flashed windows in showers routinely fail and lead to major damage. Inexpensive building and decorating materials like MDF, particleboard, veneered cabinetry, laminate counters, thinly plated metal fixtures, and wallpaper make for planned obsolescence.

Design instead with durable homogeneous materials like stone (including man-made varieties), glass and glass block, tile, terrazzo, concrete, stainless steel, and tough hardwoods. For baseboards and casings, I like to use PVC or composites such as Moisture-Shield™ (www.moistureshield.com). Wood cabinetry and trim should be a nickel's thickness off the floor to prevent water contact; furniture-leveling feet are great for letting cabinetry stay dry.

2. Slippery Floors

Shine is fine for faucets, but it's bad for bathroom floors. Glossy tile and polished stone make for slippery, unsafe floors. These materials cause lots of falls, and they're maintenance headaches, too, revealing every scratch and wearing unevenly.

Imperfections and bumps are good qualities in bathroom floors. The floor should be made of tumbled stone or tile that provides ample traction. Variation in color, texture, and size also helps to prevent falls, and it looks great, too. Use floor tiles smaller than 12×12 to increase the number of grout joints for improved traction. Shower floors need even smaller tile with lots of grout joints, both to offer traction and to conform to the floor slope. Porous tumbled stone (travertine, limestone, etc.) is an ideal bathroom-floor material, both for its traction and its low maintenance. I love designing small-stone and unglazed-tile mosaics for shower floors. Daltile® (www.daltile.com) has a reasonably priced water-jet service that allows fine details and curves to be cut in even the smallest tiles, permitting the creation of almost any image or geometry in a tile field at far less expense than hand-laid stone mosaics.

Tread cautiously when considering a wood floor. Teak, ipé, and other tropical woods might make attractive bathroom floors, but building a safe, durable wood floor for a bathroom costs a lot more than laying basic tile over backerboard and thick plywood. I still doubt wood's long-term durability, even with a good installation. As for carpet, just forget it. Water and carpet pad are a nasty brew, and don't get me started about carpet around toilets. Ick! The year 1975 was very bad for bathrooms.

3. No Natural Light

Our ancestors were so grateful to have indoor plumbing, they didn't need ambience. But nowadays, people expect a lot more from a bathroom. The tiny, damp, and dingy interior bathroom with a little round light fixture in the ceiling is old-school.

Admittedly, lack of natural light is a sin in any room, but bathrooms feel particularly creepy without natural light. Find any conceivable way to bring it into a bathroom. Use etched-glass or glass-block interior

Bathrooms feel particularly creepy without natural light. Find any conceivable way to bring it into a bathroom.

windows to carry in light from an adjoining room that has exterior windows. Use skylights. Use light tubes. Use structural glass block dropped into a hole in the floor to bring light in from the room below. Use motorized mirrors salvaged from a shuttle mission—whatever it takes. When nothing else works, use a trompe l'oeil tile design that suggests a light source exists, or paint a sun and clouds on the ceiling. I've used these tricks and more besides.

4. Boring Tile

Daunted by seemingly unlimited choices, too many people just go with a tried-and-true blanket of 4×4 white tile. It's boring, but it's safe.

Plain-Jane tile represents a lost opportunity for personal expression, or simply for visual interest. I've seen it in new houses going for over a million dollars. Taking the trouble to design with various colors or sizes costs almost nothing extra. Anything, and I mean anything, is better than a blanket of 4×4 white tile. Live a little. If you feel lost among the tile products available, keep in mind a specific design theme, and then find the tiles that execute the theme. Believe me, they're out there somewhere. But remember, a great tile design still can't overcome a leak-prone installation, which effectively makes the tile worthless.

5. Bad Math

I was once called about a just-completed tiled shower in which a sliver of cut tile ran vertically right up the middle of the wall. The installer hadn't counted before setting the tile; he and his helper started at opposite sides and met in the middle. The job had to be gutted—again.

Math is important in bathrooms because space is usually at a premium; every inch matters. Errors in math lead to glaring tile-layout problems, shower stalls and toilet alcoves that don't meet code minimums, faucet handles that bang into backsplashes (my pet peeve), oversize pedestal sinks that interfere with door clearances, large gaps between toilet tank and wall—you name it.

Measure and count over and over before materials are ordered and installed in bathrooms. Make templates whenever possible. And builders, take note: Caulk doesn't atone for the sin of bad math.

On the other hand, don't assume that because a space is small, you can't design storage solutions into it. Storage of extra toilet tissue, vanity items, and towels is important. For small bathrooms, I've designed many kinds of recessed, partly recessed, and wall-mounted cabinets; neat little drawer cabinets that sit on the floor between a toilet and a pedestal sink; and open shelves in whatever sizes and shapes seem to work for the client, given the space constraints.

6. Bathrooms in the Kitchen

People will stick powder rooms anywhere. One place is particularly egregious, though: A bathroom should not open directly into a kitchen. (Your local building code might forbid it anyway.) I will do anything to prevent a bathroom door from opening into a kitchen, or to avoid placing a toilet so that it's visible from the kitchen. No one working with food or enjoying food wants to be reminded where baked ziti goes in the end.

7. Toilets Facing the Door

You know how those little push-button door locks sometimes don't catch? It always happens when Uncle Elmer comes for a visit. Don't place a toilet facing the bathroom door. How embarrassing.

In a small bathroom, the toilet should be perpendicular to the doorway and visually screened. For instance, use simple wood screens or semitranslucent panels such as

etched glass to suggest some degree of privacy for this, the most intimate of personal tasks. My favorite solution for setting off a toilet area is a thick wood panel with an open-work design or interesting veneering. The panel needs to rest on stainless-steel furniture glides or round doorstops with the rubber pulled out so that the wood doesn't take up water through the end grain. At the same time, avoid entirely walled-in toilets in minimum code widths (usually 30 in.). People hate them, and inevitably the fan roars loudly within. A toilet stall is ideal at 36 in. to 42 in. wide, with 27 in. to 30 in. of clear space in front of the toilet.

Speaking of fans, the best advice is to vent quickly and quietly. Building codes require fart fans (this is a legitimate term in the building trades, universally understood and never confused with any other kind of fan), so builders grudgingly buy cheap $25 fans that roar like jet engines. They are attached to cheap flex duct. Effective cfm: 6. But the actual cfm is zero, since no one turns on the fan except the building inspector. For bathroom-specific venting, Panasonic (www.panasonic.com) fans are dead quiet and long-lasting. Remote blowers like those from Fantech™ (www.fantech.net) are also an option.

Patrick Sutton's Austin-based design/build firm specializes in kitchens and baths (www.suttondesign.com), and his law practice focuses on construction law (www.jpatricksuttonlaw.com).

Anything, and I mean anything, is better than a blanket of 4×4 white tile.

I will do anything to prevent a bathroom door from opening into a kitchen, or to avoid placing a toilet so that it's visible from the kitchen.

Plumbing a Basement Bathroom

■ BY MIKE GUERTIN

Adding a bathroom in a basement might sound like a complicated project, but the plumbing part of the job isn't much different from any above-grade bath. It's simple and straightforward to bring in the small-diameter supply lines for hot and cold water. Cutting the slab and digging the trench for the waste lines are the tasks that set this project apart. I work with my plumber, Paul Murray, to map out the best fixture layout, and we then divide the tasks required to complete the project. I tackle the slab work, and he lays the drain and supply piping. Of course, the sewer-outlet pipe on most of my projects is above the basement-floor elevation, so we have to install a tank to collect the sewage and a pump to send it up to the level of the sewer outlet. The rough-in process takes several days for us to complete; then we can schedule the inspections.

Plan the Drain Layout First

Rather than completely breaking out the concrete slab in the prospective bathroom, I cut trenches where the drains will run. This saves me from having to move lots of broken concrete and then repour the slab. I chalk a proposed fixture layout on the concrete slab, then meet with Paul. We review options, and he recommends layout changes that minimize my work and simplify his drain- and vent-pipe arrangement. He also identifies suitable locations for the sewage-ejector tank and draws the final trench layout.

The bathroom in this project is typical and includes a toilet, a pedestal sink, and a one-piece shower stall. Other plumbed fixtures, such as a washing machine, a utility sink, a kitchen sink, and a dishwasher, can be tied in to the same drain system.

A template makes locating drains easier. During layout, I make a cardboard template for the drain locations. Marks on the template are registered to marks on the adjacent walls. When it's time to place the drain flange, I put the template back in its spot. I've found that it's easier to cut the slab exactly rather than remove and then repour the entire area. Chalklines guide the sawcuts.

Everything Flows Downhill to a Tank

The key to a basement plumbing system is a tank with a pump that raises gray water and sewage to the main waste line, where gravity can take over. To keep everything flowing properly to the sewage tank, the drain lines from the fixtures should be pitched ¼ in. over a 12-in. run. Here, the fixture farthest from the tank, the toilet, determines the tank's vertical position.

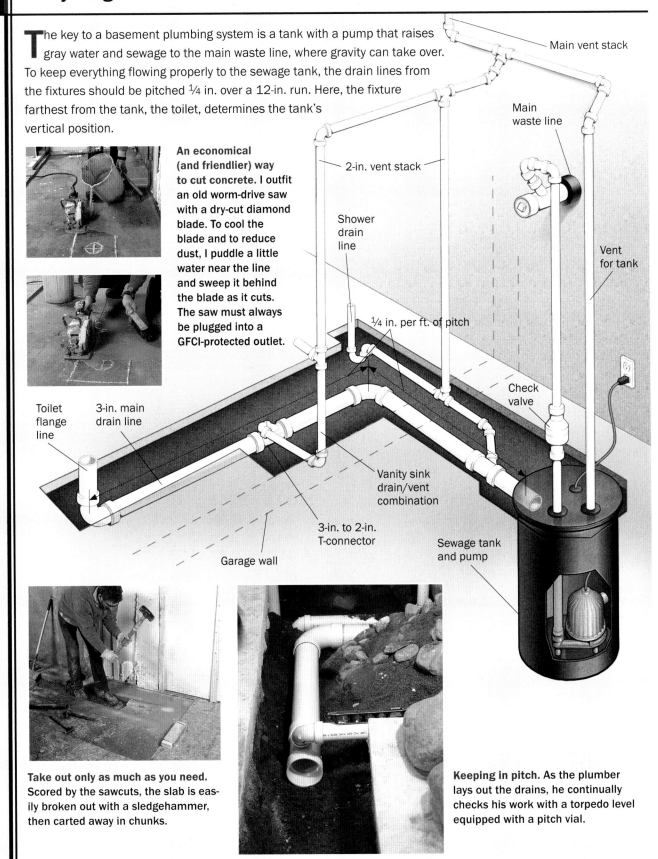

An economical (and friendlier) way to cut concrete. I outfit an old worm-drive saw with a dry-cut diamond blade. To cool the blade and to reduce dust, I puddle a little water near the line and sweep it behind the blade as it cuts. The saw must always be plugged into a GFCI-protected outlet.

Main vent stack

Main waste line

2-in. vent stack

Shower drain line

Vent for tank

¼ in. per ft. of pitch

Check valve

Toilet flange line

3-in. main drain line

Vanity sink drain/vent combination

3-in. to 2-in. T-connector

Sewage tank and pump

Garage wall

Take out only as much as you need. Scored by the sawcuts, the slab is easily broken out with a sledgehammer, then carted away in chunks.

Keeping in pitch. As the plumber lays out the drains, he continually checks his work with a torpedo level equipped with a pitch vial.

A Saw and a Sledgehammer Open the Floor

Before I start breaking up the concrete slab, I make cardboard templates of the drain-riser positions for the shower and the toilet. The templates register to the adjacent wall plates or wall layout lines, so after the slab is removed and the trench is dug, Paul has a guide for installing the drains.

The largest drainpipe will be 3 in. dia., but the trenches need to be wide enough to be shoveled out. I usually make them 10 in. to 12 in. wide to leave extra working room for fittings. To cut the slab, I use an old worm-drive saw fitted with a $40 dry-cut diamond blade; it must be plugged into a GFCI-protected outlet. The blade cuts only 2½ in. into the slab, which typically is 3 in. to 5 in. thick, but that's deep enough to give me a good, clean fracture line. A gas-powered concrete saw would cut all the way through the slab, but the exhaust inside a poorly ventilated basement would be overwhelming and would migrate into the living space above.

As the saw cuts, I flood the blade with water to cool it, as well as to speed the cut and to minimize dust. I pour a puddle of water on the floor and use a brush to sweep it to the rear of the blade. The blade draws the water forward into the cutting action. The water can be pushed back into the blade until it becomes thick slurry. After every few feet of cutting, I collect the slurry in a bucket or a shop vacuum and start a fresh puddle.

A few whacks with a 10-lb. sledgehammer crack the concrete between the sawcuts; I use a prybar to pop out pieces of the slab. Once a hole is started, the pieces come out easily. A word of caution: Some slabs are placed over plastic vapor retarders. When I encounter them, I try to be careful not to damage the plastic. I slice it down the middle of the trench and fold back the sides so that I can reuse it when backfilling.

Sewage Ejector: the Guts of the System

The sewage-ejector pump sits inside a plastic tank. It has a float-controlled switch that activates the pump when the sewage level reaches the discharge height. The sewage is pumped up and out through a 2-in.-dia. pipe to the main waste line, where the sewage flows naturally (due to gravity) rather than under pressure. A check valve mounted on the discharge pipe prevents the sewage in the discharge pipe from flowing back into the tank. In the event of a pump failure or a maintenance check, the pipe can be disconnected beneath the check valve, and the sewage inside the pipe above the valve will not leak out.

Many pumps, including the one I installed, can be serviced only by removing the tank cover and disconnecting the drain. My plumber recommends a pump by Liberty Pumps® (www.libertypumps.com) with a cover-mounted panel (see the photo below) that allows easier access to the switch. All ejector pumps are powered by regular household current; the power cord plugs into any nearby GFCI-protected outlet. The cost for a tank and pump can run from $300 to $900.

Patching the Slab Is a Small but Intensive Job

Once the drains are in place and I've backfilled, I like to compact the fill with water (1); any resulting low spots are filled and compacted again. Before I pour concrete (2), I isolate the drain risers with a wrap of cardboard, which gives me room to adjust the drain after the concrete is set. After mixing a small, stiff batch of concrete and packing it into the trench with a wooden float (3), I finish by running a vibrator (I use an Arkie Wall Banger) on a nylon cutting board (4) and, finally, by using a magnesium float and a steel trowel.

Everything Flows Downhill, So Pitch the Trench Accordingly

I use a 3×3 (3-in.-dia. by 3-in.-dia.) elbow fitting to establish the starting depth at the farthest point in the drain run from the ejector tank—in this case, the toilet (see the drawing on p. 58). To accommodate the 3-in.-dia. elbow, I start the bottom of the trench about 4 in. below the bottom of the slab. This leaves enough space above the drainpipe for the slab to be repoured to its full thickness. The trench needs to be pitched at ¼ in. per ft. I use a 6-ft. level with a pitch vial to gauge the slope as I'm digging. Any tangent trenches from incoming fixture drains need to be sloped at the same pitch, starting where they meet the main trench level. The area directly beneath the shower drain needs to be dug several inches deeper than the trench level to accommodate the trap.

The drain line terminates at the sewage-collection tank. These tanks are usually made of thick plastic and have an inlet hole drilled in the side. The pit for the tank needs to be excavated deep enough so that the bottom of the inlet hole matches the bottom of the trench. This level might cause the top of the tank to be beneath the slab level if the drain runs are long. It's important to let the trench level establish the level of the tank and not just position the tank flush with the top of the slab, or there might not be enough pitch in the drainpipes for the sewage to flow properly. On this project, the tank top needed to be 2½ in. below slab level.

Don't Forget the Vent Lines

It takes me half a day to break out the slab and to dig the trenches. Then Paul returns to install the drains. Using the cardboard templates, he dry-fits, then glues together the pipes and fittings, running them into the sewage tank. A rubber bushing seals the pipe to the tank.

Basement Bath without Cutting the Floor

Saniflo® bathroom systems (www.saniflo.com) eliminate the need to break up the basement slab. Rather than running beneath the floor, 2-in.-dia. drainpipes connect the sink, shower, or toilet to a floor-mounted tank with an ejector pump (see the photo below); the pipes can run above floor level, either behind the finished walls or on the surface. The pump and its tank can be recessed into a framed wall with an access-panel for future pump-service. The shower pan is raised 6 in. to 7 in. off the finished floor, and the price is a bit steep (a toilet and pump combo alone costs about $800). With headroom at a premium in the bathroom, I could afford to lose only 2 in. of a typical shower-stall floor.

Isolate the tank lid, but not the tank. I use a ring of cardboard as a form around the sewage tank's lid so that the repoured patch sits on top of the tank rim but doesn't interfere with the removal of the lid. In some regions, seasonally high water tables can lift the tank right out of its hole if it's not secured.

Once all the pipes have been laid, we backfill about three quarters of the way around them to keep the pipes from shifting. The top of the trench is left exposed for the rough-plumbing inspection. If I'm working in an area that has a high water table, I fill the tank to the inlet, or I weight it with rocks to prevent it from floating if the groundwater level rises.

While the drain lines are exposed, Paul installs the plumbing vents. Proper venting is required by code and is necessary for the drains to work. The vents equalize air pressure inside drains and prevent traps from being sucked dry. Ideally, we run a vent pipe to the exterior of the building or tap into an existing vent pipe in the floor above. A vent pipe can be run through a wall above, can be concealed in a closet, or can be run on an exterior wall. On this project, we tapped into a vent pipe on the first floor as part of a more-extensive remodeling project. Although air-admittance valves are an alternative for venting difficult locations and can be used to vent fixtures in a basement bathroom, don't use them to vent the sewage tank itself. We have run into problems with both odors and poor pump flow when we've used air valves in the past. Pumps perform much better when they are vented atmospherically.

Leave Yourself Options after Patching the Slab

After the inspector's approval, I backfill around the pipes. The cardboard templates are used to position the shower, sink, and toilet risers precisely. While the backfill is still loose, the pipes are easy to shift a little to match the templates.

I then wrap the risers with strips of corrugated cardboard or surround them with a piece of larger-diameter pipe. The toilet stub, for instance, is left unglued to the fitting below so that it can be trimmed later to match the finished-flooring level when the toilet flange is mounted. The spacer keeps the concrete away from the pipe so that the stub later can be cut to length and glued. The spacers also leave a little wiggle room for fine-tuning the drain risers to match the fixture outlets. This is especially important when you're installing a one-piece shower.

Once the pipes are positioned, I flood the area several times with water to ensure that the backfill is packed tightly around them. The water helps to consolidate the soil and to fill in any gaps. The soil often settles when it's flooded, so I add more dirt flush with the bottom of the old slab and then flood the area again. Finally, I cover the trench with 6-mil plastic as a vapor retarder and tape it to the existing plastic vapor retarder when it is present.

The slab patch usually doesn't require enough concrete to warrant bringing in a ready-mix truck, so I either mix concrete in a wheelbarrow by hand or in a portable mixer. I mix the concrete to a stiff consistency and then pack it into the trench. Next, I run a concrete vibrator over a plastic cutting board and finish up by going over the surface with a magnesium float and a steel trowel.

After the concrete cures for a couple of days, Paul returns for a few hours to install the supply tubing and to mount the shower mixing valve. I install the subfloor panels, the drywall, and the finished flooring before Paul's final visit to set the toilet and install the sink.

Mike Guertin (www.mikeguertin.com) *is a builder and remodeling contractor from East Greenwich, Rhode Island.* **Paul Murray**, *a second-generation master plumber and mechanical contractor in Johnston, Rhode Island, contributed to this article.*

Installing a Shower Niche

■ BY JANE AEON

Tired of bumping into that wire shower caddy hanging awkwardly off the showerhead? Do you hate the unsightly clutter at the edges of your bathtub? Organize your shower or bath space by building a niche that offers convenient storage and a charming sense of bathroom design. In recent years, these small recessed spaces have become popular components of bathtub surrounds and showers. In fact, all the bathrooms I tile these days are outfitted with some sort of niche.

Niche Size and Location Affect Function

Before determining where on the wall the niche should go, decide the size that would be most useful for your shower niche. I often build 12-in. by 12-in. niches, but I find that 14-in.-tall niches can accommodate oversize shampoo bottles a little better. Don't let standard stud spacing be the sole determinant in the size of a niche. The benefit of building a niche, as opposed to installing a prefabricated one (see "Prefab Niches Have Their Place" on p. 69), is that you can easily create spaces of all shapes and sizes.

Determine the Location of the Niche with a Story Pole

By modifying the framing in a bathroom wall with blocking, you can build custom-size niches in almost any location on the wall. First, though, create a story pole (I use my aluminum straightedge) by marking off tiles spaced for ¼-in. grout joints. Held vertically against the wall, this layout tool helps determine where to frame the niche by ensuring that it won't be bordered by awkwardly sized tiles.

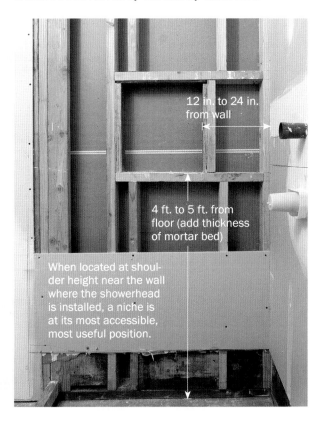

12 in. to 24 in. from wall

4 ft. to 5 ft. from floor (add thickness of mortar bed)

When located at shoulder height near the wall where the showerhead is installed, a niche is at its most accessible, most useful position.

Once you've decided on the size of the niche and a general location on the wall that balances accessibility and aesthetics, fine-tune its position with a story pole to be sure that the niche opening lines up with the grout joints. Transfer the layout marks from the story pole to the studs to orient the framing of the niche and then again on the backerboard once it's installed to guide the tile layout.

In the project featured here, the architect and builder positioned and framed the niche slightly above the height of a nearby vanity. I had to increase the width of the grout joints so that the tiles would align properly on the wall.

Frame the Niche Larger Than Necessary

To frame most niche openings, I nail horizontal 2× blocking between the existing studs.

Flash the Wall and Niche to Prevent Water Intrusion

In many parts of the country, greenboard drywall doesn't meet code for use as a tile substrate due to its poor performance in wet conditions. Here, I use it behind cement backerboard, which meets code, as a means of building out the shower wall. I then can install an attractive quarter-round edge tile at the thickened edge of the shower, where the tile ends and the wallboard begins. Its use, however, puts an even stronger emphasis on proper waterproofing measures.

Flexible Flashing Seals the Niche

I place a thin, self-adhesive flexible-flashing membrane in the niche, being sure to lap each strip at least an inch over the one below so that any water is shed down the wall rather than being trapped inside it (photo 1). I like Protecto Wrap® (see "Sources" on p. 69) flexible flashing because it's easy to work with, and, like other flexible flashings, it seals securely around nail and staple penetrations.

A Vapor Retarder Keeps the Framing and Wallboard Dry

I use Aquabar® by Fortifiber™ (see "Sources" on p. 69), which is two layers of kraft paper laminated with asphalt. I attach it directly to the face of the greenboard or studs with staples (photo 2), making sure to double-layer each corner for added protection. The bottom strip of niche flashing should lap over the vapor retarder (photo 3).

Caulk Seals Both Membranes

I cut out the niche opening and seal the edges with silicone caulk (photo 4) before securing them with staples.

Line the Niche with Backerboard and Mud

Creating a solid, uniform substrate is crucial. After cutting and screwing ½-in. cement backerboard to the wall, I line the top, back, and sides of the niche with scraps. Mudding the bottom is the last preparation step.

Don't Screw in the Niche's Back Panel
Measure, cut, and place a few beads of silicone caulk on the back of the niche's back panel before installing it. This piece is also held in place by the pressure of the niche's top and side pieces, which are secured with screws.

Tape All the Joints at Once
Once all the backerboard is firmly in place, I cover each joint in the shower with mesh tape and a coat of thinset. When the thinset has cured, I knock down any imperfections and high spots with a sanding block.

Slope the Bottom to Shed Water
Trowel a ½-in. layer of mortar in the bottom of the niche, and use a level to make sure it has a slight pitch. Slant the bottom of the niche just enough so that water flows out of it, but not so much that bars of soap and bottles of shampoo slide out. I aim for a ⅛-in. slope over 3 in.

Story Pole Keeps Tile Layout on Course

On a typical project, the tile layout is determined when I first begin framing the niche. I use the story pole as a reference to draw layout lines on the wall. Then I lay tile as I would on any other vertical tiling project.

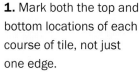

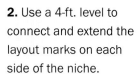

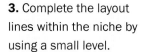

Transfer Layout Marks to the Wall

I make layout marks on each side of the niche with a mechanical pencil for absolute accuracy.

1. Mark both the top and bottom locations of each course of tile, not just one edge.

2. Use a 4-ft. level to connect and extend the layout marks on each side of the niche.

3. Complete the layout lines within the niche by using a small level.

Secure Top Tiles with Short Sticks

Thanks to careful layout, the niche lands nicely in the tiled shower wall. To hold up the niche's top tiles while the thinset cures, I wedge two vertical pieces of scrap wood under one flat, horizontal piece.

But each installation has subtle differences. In some 2×4 walls, the existing framing is shallower than 3½ in. In these cases, I use ¼-in.-thick backerboard in the back of the niche instead of ½-in.-thick backerboard to gain as much usable space as possible. When working with a 2×6 wall, I have to choose between creating a deep recess or padding it out with plywood or backerboard to decrease its depth.

No matter what type of framing you have to deal with, always frame the niche at least ¾ in. to 1 in. larger than you want the final opening to be. This allows you to adjust the tile layout if necessary and also provides room for ⅛-in.-thick waterproofing membrane, ½ in. of mortar and backerboard, and the thickness of the tile. If you're using quarter-round edge tiles, as in this bath, give yourself even more room; this type of tile requires a bit more space.

A Hole in a Wet Wall Can Be Disastrous

If you're not intimidated by installing a shower niche, you should be. You're creating a hole in a wall located in the wettest area of your home. Poorly flashing and waterproofing this recess can easily lead to mold and rot problems.

In this bathroom, the architect specified quarter-round edge tiles around the niche and along the edges of the shower. To accommodate this detail, I attached backerboard over greenboard to fur out the shower perimeter from the bathroom wall. Otherwise, I would attach the backerboard directly to the studs. I use three waterproofing products in and around niches (see "Flash the Wall Niche to Prevent Water Intrusion" on p. 66), and their installation is the same with each type of wall assembly.

Create a Solid Substrate in the Niche

I like using standard cement backerboard in bathrooms because tiles don't set up on it nearly as quickly as with fiber-cement backerboard. That means I can make minor adjustments to the tile as I go. However, I usually use whatever product that I have excess of to avoid wasting material.

When installing backerboard in a shower niche, I install the back panel with silicone, not screws. By using silicone, I eliminate the possibility of damaging the drywall on the opposite side of the bathroom wall.

Once the cement backerboard is in place, I cover all the joints with mesh tape buried in thinset. I finish the mud work by troweling a ½-in. layer of mortar in the bottom of the niche, slightly sloped to the outside edge so that water can drain from the niche instead of pooling inside it.

Lay Tile as if Working on a Regular Wall

Tiling a wall with a well-appointed niche is done like any other wall-tiling project. When working in the shower niche, I install a row of tiles on the bottom of the niche first, followed by a course of tiles in the back of the niche; these tiles are held flush to the tops of the bottom tiles. Applying the niche's side tiles and edge treatment, if called for, completes the course.

In some bathrooms, I like to replace the bottom tiles with a piece of solid stone for a dramatic yet elegant look. The installation sequence is the same, but the visual interest is certainly not.

Jane Aeon is a tile contractor in Berkeley, California, and Oklahoma City, Oklahoma.

Sources

Ceramic Tile Specialties
704-957-8594
www.getproform.com
Prefab niche

Fortifiber Building Systems Group
800-773-4777
www.fortifiber.com

Innovis Corporation
916-361-2601
www.innoviscorp.com
Prefab niche

Noble Company®
800-878-5788
www.noblecompany.com
Prefab niche

Protecto Wrap Company
800-759-9727
www.protectowrap.com

Prefab Niches Have Their Place

I often use prefabricated niches when a homeowner or architect calls for a more elaborate design. There's simply no other way to get a niche with a steepled or arched top secured into a wall as quickly.

Prefabricated niches (see "Sources" above right) eliminate some of the steps called for when framing a niche from scratch. There's no need to mortar the bottom of the niche because prefab niches have a slope built into their form. There are fewer joints to tape and mud, and waterproofing measures are generally less stringent because prefab niches are solid, one-piece units.

However, prefabricated niches have some limitations. Installation of certain models can be finicky if a wall's framing is warped or out of square. And although these niches come in a variety of sizes, they don't offer nearly as much adjustability in regard to tile layout as a framed niche.

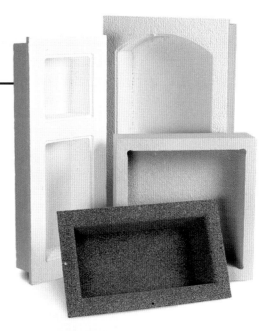

Prefab niches

Glass-Block Shower on a Curve

■ BY TOM MEEHAN

It wasn't long ago that shower stalls were made to serve one purpose: getting you clean. Color choice was the only real aesthetic concern; size and shape were considered matters of utility and efficiency.

Now, people think of showering as an important part of the day, both physically and mentally. The small dungeons of the past are being replaced with functional works of art. To this end, I think that glass block blows away most other shower options.

Glass-block showers are a great way to let in some light and to provide a sense of openness and freedom, even in a small bathroom. Glass blocks offer tremendous design flexibility, yet the subtle visual distortion of glass affords full privacy. No more dungeons.

This shower-stall alternative lets in the light, offers privacy, and makes a small space feel roomy.

New Accessories Make for an Easier Installation

If you wanted a glass-block shower a decade ago, I would have told you to find a mason—and for good reason. Unless you have experience, glass blocks are hard to keep straight and plumb. The best that beginners could hope to accomplish was a couple of courses at a time, and they would likely still struggle to keep the work in line until the mortar set up.

With just one change in design from a basic wall supported on all four sides—whether it's the addition of a curved surface, a wall that stops short of the ceiling, or one that is unsupported on one end—the project becomes more complicated. Some projects, such as the shower that's featured here, combine all these complications and then some.

Now, though, glass-block manufacturers like Pittsburgh Corning™ (see "Sources" on p. 76) are taking a bit of the fear out of the process by offering helpful installation accessories. The cornerstone of these accessories is the glass-block spacer. These pieces of plastic lock each block in place as it is installed, and are left in place and covered by grout. More work can be done at one time, and the blocks don't shift or slip out of place as easily.

Don't get me wrong: Glass-block installations still take patience and careful attention to detail. But I hope these installation accessories combined with my hard-learned installation tricks will help to ease what was once a much-steeper learning curve.

Build the Curb with Concrete Blocks

A straight shower curb can be built by doubling up 2×4s and nailing them to the floor, but curves are more work. For curves, I arrange a row of glass blocks on the floor into the desired shape, trace around them, cut

A curved foundation. Landscape blocks are used to create a curved foundation.

Waterproofed and pitched for drainage. The author uses a waterproofing membrane and slightly pitches the marble cap to achieve proper drainage.

Cut the curves. The author uses a Gemini Revolution tile saw to cut the pieces for the top of the curb.

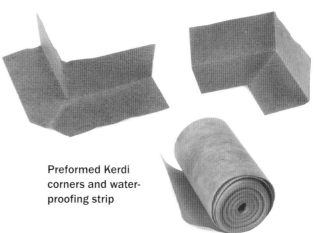

Preformed Kerdi corners and water-proofing strip

Establish the layout. The glass blocks are first laid dry and then traced with a pencil.

Prep the curb to hold the blocks. The marble cap is scarified in preparation for the thinset.

concrete landscape blocks to fit the shape, and set them in thinset. Next, I float a mortar bed for the shower floor.

Once the concrete blocks and mortar bed have set up, the curb is waterproofed. I like to wrap the curb in preparation for the 2-in. tiles used to cover the sides and the marble caps that go on top. Square shower pans can be waterproofed with a one-piece vinyl membrane like Chloraloy®, but I like the Schlüter®-Kerdi® system (see "Sources" on p. 76; bottom right photo on p. 71) for curved pans because the membrane can be cut into wedges and overlapped where needed to get

Mix the Mortar Stiff

Glass blocks must be installed using a special glass-block mortar; don't be tempted to use any other products in a pinch. The lime in this powdered mortar mix is hazardous to your health if inhaled, so wear a respirator. I start with a 50-lb. bag of glass-block mortar in a small plastic mortar tub, then I slowly add water as I work the mortar with a small mixing hoe. The mortar should be fairly stiff; too loose, and the blocks will slide. To be on the safe side, I like to get the mortar close to the right consistency, then dribble a little water at a time into the tub using a grouting sponge.

The curb is coated with thinset, then the blocks are set in a thick bed of glass-block mortar.

Keep the first course sturdy and level. This first course is crucial, and each block is checked for level.

Lock it up. Glass-block spacers lock the blocks in place and keep the grout joint consistent.

around tight curves. Because the Kerdi membrane is easily damaged, I don't set it on the shower floor until I'm done installing the glass blocks.

Before tiling the concrete-block curb, I set the waterproofing membrane for the curb in a layer of thinset. Because the curb will be visible, I cap it with marble pitched slightly toward the inside of the shower for proper drainage (see the top middle photo on p. 71). To help get the marble overhang right, I tile the sides of the curb before capping it.

I cut the curved cap pieces on a Gemini Revolution tile saw (see "Sources" on p. 76) because its 10-in.-dia. ring-shaped diamond blade allows me to follow a tighter inside or outside curve than I could cut with a standard wet saw (see the bottom middle photo on p. 71). A standard wet saw can also be used, but you have to make a series of straight cuts up to the curved line, then remove the waste with tile nippers.

After the marble cap has been installed and has set up for a day, I dry-lay the glass blocks in place to make sure they line up properly (see the top left photo on the facing page). Once I'm happy with the layout, I trace the outline of the blocks with a pencil. Don't use a permanent marker here because the marks

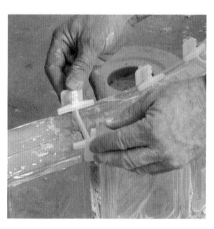

Be aware. Both the straight run glass-block spacers (left) and those for curves (right) look very similar.

Panel anchors tie the glass blocks to the wall.

Expansion strips are used where the blocks meet a wall, ceiling, or header.

Joint reinforcement is used at the same horizontal joint as panel anchors.

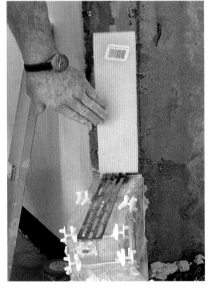

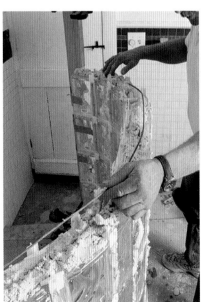

could be visible once the glass is installed. After the layout is traced onto the marble cap, I scarify the cap with a diamond blade in an angle grinder (see the top right photo on p. 72). This allows the thinset to lock into the surface of the marble cap.

Take Extra Time to Set the First Course

The first course of glass blocks sets the stage for the entire installation. Take as much time as necessary to get the blocks strongly adhered and perfectly level in both directions before moving on.

I skim-coat the curb with thinset, then set the first course of blocks on a thick bed of glass-block mortar (see the top left photo on p. 73). The thinset and mortar lock together as they dry. Check each block for level (see the top right photo on p. 73), and shim with tile spacers where necessary. It's better to use too much mortar and have it squeeze out than to use too little and risk voids.

Use glass-block spacers. They establish a consistent ¼-in. grout joint and lock the blocks in place. There are two different spacers for this project. One is for straight runs; the other is for curves (see the bottom right photos on p. 73). Be careful, though. Both spacers look similar, and they are easy to install upside down accidentally.

Reinforce as You Rise

For this job, I had an entry opening on one end of the shower wall, and the glass blocks also stopped short of the ceiling. Without using the manufacturer's panel anchors, rebar, and block spacers, the wall would have been pretty shaky. Take the time to reinforce the wall where recommended.

Sixteen-inch-long stainless-steel panel anchors tie the glass blocks to the walls (see the top photo at left). The anchors must be bent into an L-shape. The short leg should be about 4 in. long and installed every two vertical feet.

A Pair of Levels Keeps Things in Line

Glass blocks around door openings often shift during assembly. To keep things in line, I clamp a long level to the face of the glass blocks, then clamp a short level to the long level so that I can check for plumb in two directions as I work. As new blocks are placed, I fasten them to the levels with painter's tape to keep them from shifting.

Twist off the tabs and clean. The tabs can be taken off after the blocks have set up but before the cement cures.

Always use sanded grout for large joints. It is the strongest choice.

Sources

Gemini Saw Company
310-891-0288
www.geminisaw.com
Revolution tile saw

Noble Company
800-878-5788
www.noblecompany.com
Chloraloy

Pittsburgh Corning™
800-624-2120
www.pittsburghcorning.com

Schlüter Company
800-472-4588
www.schluter.com
Kerdi system

Wherever glass blocks will abut a wall, a ceiling, or a header, a ¼-in. poly expansion strip must be installed (see the middle photo on p. 74). Lap the strip over the stainless-steel panel anchor. There's no need for expansion strips under the first course.

I place panel-reinforcement strips in a bed of glass-block mortar at the same horizontal joints that require panel anchors (see the bottom photo on p. 74). For curved walls, I cut the strips in half, bend them to the desired radius, and lay the halves side by side.

Clean, Grout, and Clean Again

The final stages of a glass-block installation are always the most gratifying. Remove excess mortar, pack the joints with grout, and clean the glass to a glistening shine.

The spacer tabs can be taken off after the blocks have set up a bit, usually about 2 hours to 3 hours (see the top left photo above). Don't wait until the cement cures, though. The excess mortar behind the tabs must be cleaned off before it hardens completely.

The strongest choice for finishing large joints is sanded grout. Pack the grout into the joints, and scrape off the excess before wiping the entire surface with a sponge and

Remove the haze. Firmly buff the blocks with a cotton cloth.

cool, clean water. After the grout has firmed up a bit, remove the grout haze by firmly buffing the blocks with a cotton cloth.

Tom Meehan is a second-generation tile installer who has been installing tile for more than 35 years. Tom lives with his wife, Lane, and their four sons in Harwich, Massachusetts, where they own Cape Cod Tileworks.

Shower-Door Sampler

■ BY MATTHEW TEAGUE

More often than not, the shower door is the first thing you notice when you walk into a bathroom. Unfortunately, this first thing you see is most often the last thing considered in a bathroom's design. Choosing a shower door might not be the first design decision made, but its prominence within the space demands that it ought not be left for last. Whatever type of shower you have—a simple tub enclosure or an expansive tiled-in shower room—there are numerous ways to contain shower overspray, and it pays to explore all the options.

Ten years ago, the bulk of the market consisted of premade stock doors, many of them sliders. However, the market has shifted, and the attention on custom designs is greater than ever. Manufacturers have responded by creating efficient production methods, which demand a lead time as short as five days to make a custom-looking piece without the custom price tag. What this means for you is a greater selection of doors to choose from, but also a more complex decision-making process. Here, I'll save you some of the trouble and explore the most popular door options, their strengths, their weaknesses, general costs, and caveats.

Select an Operating Style That Fits the Bathroom Layout

While sliding and swinging doors are the most common styles, bifold, curved, and neo-angle designs also have their place. Armed with the footprint of the shower and the height requirements, you first must figure out what type of operating style suits your bathroom best. In general, the larger the shower, the more enclosure options you'll have. In small bathrooms, you'll be limited to doors that need little space when they're opened and closed.

Subtle, but suitable. In the past decade, shower doors with clear or slightly obscure glass have been homeowners' leading choice, representing about 95 percent of the market.

Sliding Doors

Don't let memories of a rickety 1960s slider—which was prone to leaking, jamming, and jumping out of its tracks—scare you off. New models, like Basco's® 3400 unit (see the photo at right), not only work smoothly but also come in a wide range of styles with endless glass options. Units range from those with one fixed door and one sliding door to those with multiple sliding doors, which allow a wider entryway to the shower. While sliders are still used mostly on tub/shower combinations, newer models, like MTI's Teutonic (see the photo on the facing page), look great on stand-alone shower stalls.

Traditionally, sliders are framed units, but newer models come in sleek semiframeless designs. Sliders referred to as "frameless" typically describe only the panels; there has to be some kind of structure to hold the door in place. Most frameless sliders have top and side frames of some kind, even if they're minimal. Thicker and heavier glass requires more substantial framework. The top of the door is usually guided with rollers or bearings that are hidden seamlessly in the frame. The clunky lower tracks of old, which filled with water and soap scum over time, are no longer an issue. Lower tracks require only a small channel outfitted with a center guide to keep the panels moving on the correct plane.

What to Look For

Avoid doors with multiple grooves on the lower track. Although most tracks have weep holes, the potential for water collection exists if the holes are not at the

A sliding door for the modern bath. This shower door, made by Basco, represents the custom appeal of a factory-made door that has a relatively low price tag. The sleek frame, with an oil-rubbed bronze finish, holds $3/16$ -in.-thick glass. The door costs roughly $550 (as shown).

Shower Doors May Vary, but Materials Don't

No matter what type of door you choose, you'll find that they're all constructed of similar materials. Shower doors and surrounds are made of some type of safety glass—plastic, glass, or a combination of the two. Plastic is the least expensive see-through option, but it comes at a cost. Plastic is easily scratched, and it tends to display wear and tear much more prominently than does true glass.

Although there is no industry standard, shower doors range in thickness from $3/16$ in. up to $1/2$ in. Thick glass panels offer a

lowest point of the track. Smooth surfaces where water runs directly back into the basin are best; they're easier to keep clean. Make sure the door you choose comes with or allows you to attach towel bars where you want them—outside the shower, inside the shower, or both.

Installation Notes

The installation of most sliding units can be DIY as long as you've got enough helping hands to manage the weight of the door. Be sure to check the opening for square before you choose a unit, and make sure the framework can be adjusted easily in out-of-plumb situations. Tracks and frames that abut the walls or basin should be caulked with silicone on the outer side but left open on the inside so that water can weep back into the shower.

Roll on. The Teutonic by MTI, with its exposed barnlike rail and rollers, is nothing short of an architectural expression that turns a simple sliding door into a bathroom focal point. This shower door is outside the average price range for sliders and can cost several thousand dollars ($3,600 for a 60-in. unit).

more substantial appearance and evoke a greater sense of quality, especially in frameless designs. However, thick glass, which can increase overall costs, requires hardware that has been engineered to handle lots of weight.

Glass can be purchased in a range of styles: clear, tinted or colored, textured or patterned, and sandblasted or custom-etched.

Trying to keep clear-glass doors clean, however, has scared away many buyers. In just the past few years, manufacturers have begun treating clear doors with a coating such as Basco's AquaGlide®, which works much like Rain-X® to make cleaning easier and less frequent.

The frames and hardware used on shower doors are generally made of anodized alumi-

Swinging Doors

Swinging shower doors open just like the front door on your house, using either a traditional hinge or a pivot at the top and bottom of the door. The hardware on pivoting doors is usually less obtrusive, but choosing the right hinge is a good opportunity to complement or play off the fixtures and hardware in the bathroom.

Shower doors are generally 24 in. to 36 in. wide and open outward, so make sure that adjacent cabinets, toilets, or vanities won't interfere with the swing of the door. Many models also swing inward 10° to 20°, making it easier to reach in and adjust the water temperature before you step into the shower. Swinging doors are seldom a good choice for tub/shower combinations.

What to Look For

How a door closes—with a magnetic seal, a gasket, or a catch—is a matter of preference. Whenever possible, try out the shower door in person before making a purchase. Because the doors swing outward, take a close look at the method used to prevent water on the open door from dripping onto the floor. Most employ a vinyl sweep or a channel-style drip edge—they can be almost invisible—but make sure the drip edge will last for the long haul or can be replaced easily. If you're tall, make sure the header (if there is one) is high enough so that you can step into the shower without ducking your head. Always remember that you get what you pay for. Cheap swinging doors are cheap for a reason.

Installation Notes

The actual installation is fairly straightforward, but measurements and pilot holes must be spot-on for the door to function as it should. Whether you do it yourself or hire an installer, make sure that out-of-plumb walls are addressed, either by having the glass cut to fit or by adjusting the mount used to tie the glass to the wall. Depending on the size of the unit and the thickness of the glass, heavier units may require extra blocking in the wall.

Frameless doors highlight hardware. The clean simplicity of a frameless swinging door allows hardware to shine, playing off other bathroom fixtures. This door, by Kohler, costs $820.

A framed door has mass that evokes strength. The bronze-finished frame on this swinging door adds a sense of quality and durability to the bathroom. The cost is typical of a quality door, at roughly $1,600 (as shown, including surround).

num, with applied finishes that match most any fixture you can buy, including brushed nickel, polished aluminum, bronze, oil-rubbed bronze, gold, and chrome. A few low-end models have acrylic frames, while metal hardware for a few high-end systems comes in brushed or plated brass, stainless steel, or powder-coated aluminum. Hinge materials range from small aluminum hinges to full-length versions in brass or stainless steel. As you would imagine, you'll pay a premium for hardware made of brass or stainless steel.

The Best Door Complements the Bath

Whether it's a bifold, swinging, or curved shower door, more and more homeowners are opting for frameless surrounds. While there's no functional advantage, frameless and semiframeless designs offer less distraction, leaving unobstructed views that help highlight a sweeping cathedral ceiling or make a small bathroom seem larger. Framed shower enclosures, however, are easier to manufacture, and they are usually less fussy to install against out-of-plumb walls. Framed doors create a focal point and help direct the eye to what's within the frame, be it an etched-glass door or a sheet of clear glass that showcases high-end fixtures or exceptional tilework.

Although there are exceptions, frameless designs are generally the more expensive type of shower door. Just be sure to take a close look at what you're really buying. Many shower surrounds that are marketed as frameless actually have frames on everything but the shower door. Why pay for a frameless design that looks just like a framed model?

While some shower doors (framed or frameless) can be hinged directly to the wall and span the entire opening, most feature at least one stationary panel fastened to the shower wall. In these cases, hinges can be

Frameless design varies. A door marketed as a frameless door (left) may actually be incorporated into a framed enclosure (below), drastically changing its look.

Shower Shields Supply Simple Protection

Long common in Europe, shower shields lend a clean, open look that is just starting to catch on in the States. A shower screen, as the shields are sometimes called, consists of one or more panels that span about two-thirds of the width of the shower opening and contain the majority of the water. One panel is fixed to the wall, and in most cases, a partial panel is hinged to the stationary one. The hinged panel folds out of the way so that you can enter easily or swing it out of the way when you're bathing. While most shields are designed for use on tub/shower combinations, you can find models for shower stalls as well.

Because a shield won't catch all the overspray from a shower, it's not a good choice for every situation. You wouldn't want to use a shower shield, for instance, in a bathroom that has hardwood floors. Also, make sure that a little water won't ruin nearby fixtures.

Fixed, but functional. Shower shields offer spray protection for both shower stalls and tub/shower combinations, and they are available in fixed and hinged designs, which increase accessibility. This shield, by Kohler, is priced at $1,900.

mounted to a post that runs from floor to ceiling, to the framework of adjacent glass, or directly to the glass side panel. Avoid glass-to-glass hinges that simply clamp the glass in place. Better hinges use mounting screws that run through holes drilled in the glass. Hinges may span the entire length of the door and panel, but frameless designs usually feature only two or three small hinges. On pivoting doors, pins are attached to the top and bottom of the door and are housed in blocks. On frameless doors, the pivots are often mounted at the top and bot-

Curved and Neo-Angle Doors

Although less common, curved and neo-angle shower enclosures are another great option when there's a shortage of space in the bathroom. Corner models take up as little as a 3-ft. by 3-ft. footprint. Besides saving space, the lines of both neo-angle and curved shower doors are an easy way to lend visual interest to an otherwise rectilinear design. Neo-angle enclosures typically feature two fixed side panels and a center panel that swings open on either a hinge or a pivot. A curved shower door may open on a pivot, a hinge, or along a set of rollers that run in tracks at top and bottom— somewhat like a bypass door, except it slides with the arc of the curve. Either style can be found in framed, frameless, or semiframed designs and with similar hardware options as sliding or swinging enclosures.

What to Look For
Because the hardware mechanisms are similar, concerns are the same as with sliding or swinging doors.

Installation Notes
When purchasing a single unit—shower with enclosure included—make sure there is an easy way (as part of the unit or with trim) to compensate for walls and floors that are out of plumb. Otherwise, you'll never get an installation as seamless as you want.

A space-saving design. Neo-angle glass doors make corner-shower installations possible and reduce the reliance on valuable open space in the bath. At $625, this Kohler unit is on the lower end of the cost spectrum.

Curved construction. Curved shower doors offer the same space-saving qualities as neo-angle doors, but add quite a bit more architectural interest. Curved glass is expensive, which is reflected by the $5,000 price tag of this high-end Kohler unit.

Bifold Doors

Bifold shower doors are hinged in the middle so that, like an accordion, they fold in on each other. They are often used in small bathrooms where the space is limited, when the width of the shower opening is too tight for a traditional sliding door, or when there isn't enough room to open a swinging door. Although bifold doors have traditionally been of poor quality, better models are now made with the same materials and features as in other shower doors. They're available in framed and frameless versions, and they can be quite handsome.

What to Look For

The key to smooth action on a framed bifold door is in the guides that run in the tracks. Look for quality bearings or guides that won't wear over time. If there's a lower track, make sure it will neither trap water nor allow it to drip onto the floor.

Installation Notes

To ensure smooth operation, make sure the wall is plumb, or shim out the door to make it so. If you plan to install the door yourself, check that the mechanism or hinge holding the door to the wall can be adjusted easily.

A big door that works in a small bath. Bifold doors demand a very small footprint to operate properly, which is an asset in tiny bathrooms that are short on space. This Kohler door costs $1,500.

Secure, through and through. Hinges that clamp glass in place aren't as strong as those that use fasteners. A pilot hole in the glass allows screws to be secured into the matching leaf.

Sources

Agalite
www.agalite.com

American Shower Door
www.americanshowerdoor.com

Artistcraft
www.artistcraft.com

Basco
www.bascoshowerdoor.com

Century Bathworks®
www.centurybathworks.com

Kohler
www.kohler.com

MTI® Whirlpools
www.mtiwhirlpools.com

tom of the sidelite or wall, so pivoting doors do not require a track or frame.

Side panels mount to the wall either with channel-type extrusions, with wall-mount clamps, or with wall mounts that clamp and/or screw the glass in place. High-end installations are occasionally dado-mounted into a groove in the stone or tile that covers the shower wall.

Matthew Teague is a contributing writer for Fine Homebuilding.

Replace a Shower Mixing Valve

■ BY ED CUNHA

I do most of my plumbing work on Cape Cod, where there's no shortage of older homes, so it's pretty common for me to replace the old two-handle controls on a tub or shower with a new mixing valve.

In addition to offering the convenience of a single-lever control, a modern mixing valve uses a pressure-balancing mechanism to protect bathers from sudden temperature changes. If someone turns on the dishwasher or flushes a toilet while you're in the shower, a pressure-balanced valve instantly detects the change in water pressure and maintains the hot-to-cold mix you selected.

Here are two ways to complete the job. The first technique is to open the wall behind the plumbing and switch out the valves. The second method is to remove the tile, replace the valves, and retile. Obviously, I'd rather go with the former instead of the latter.

Ed Cunha is a plumber who lives and works on Cape Cod, Massachusetts.

The new pressure-balanced valve (facing page) provides safer, more convenient temperature control than you'll get from two handles (above).

Single-Lever Mixing Valve

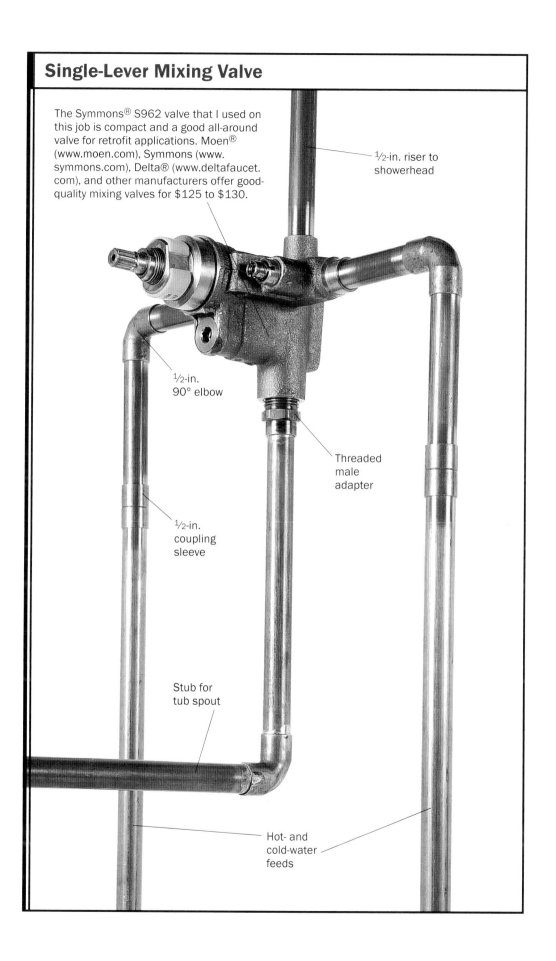

The Symmons® S962 valve that I used on this job is compact and a good all-around valve for retrofit applications. Moen® (www.moen.com), Symmons (www. symmons.com), Delta® (www.deltafaucet. com), and other manufacturers offer good-quality mixing valves for $125 to $130.

½-in. riser to showerhead

½-in. 90° elbow

Threaded male adapter

½-in. coupling sleeve

Stub for tub spout

Hot- and cold-water feeds

It's Easier to Work from the Back

1

The chrome has to come off. Pry off the cover plates that hide each handle's installation screws, then remove the screws, handles, and backing plates. In case the spout will be reused, I protect its finish with a rag as I unscrew it with Channellock® pliers.

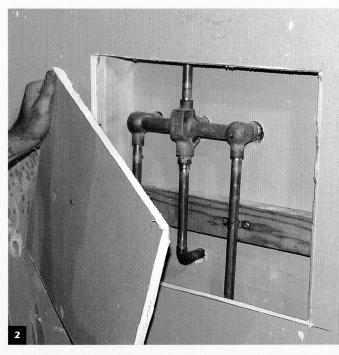

2

Cut an access panel. If there's not an access panel behind the tub's plumbing wall, you'll have to cut through the wallboard. I transfer measurements from the tiled side of the wall to the back and cut out a rectangular panel. A panel that extends from stud to stud (as shown here) is easier to patch.

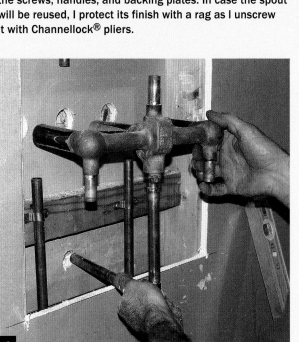

4

Lift out the old valves . . . After cutting the riser line that feeds the showerhead, I can pull the old valve free. I'm careful not to damage drywall edges.

5

. . . And make room for the new. I'll reuse the central hole for the tub spout, but I need to enlarge the hole so that it will accept the body of the new valve. I use a pair of tile nippers to clip away the tile and backerboard. The unused hot and cold holes will be covered by the goof plate.

3 **A tiny cutter for tight spaces.** A standard tubing cutter is too large to use in the wall space, so I use a mini-cutter (about $20 in most home centers) to cut the hot and cold lines that feed the old valve. I make these cuts at the same level so that I'll have an easier time fitting the new valve.

Assemble and Solder in Back, Then Finish in Front

6

Dry-fit and measure. The valve's showerhead and tub-spout pipes are in place; now I can measure for the new tubing to connect the hot and cold supply lines. I prep all mating joints with 120-grit emery cloth and a cleaning brush (inset).

7

Flux, assemble, and solder. Make sure the elbows, couplings, and short tubing sections join the new valve securely to the old lines. Clean and flux the joints, then solder with the entire assembly in place. To protect the valve's washers, I open the valve before soldering.

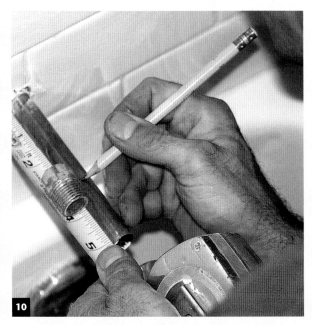

10

Prepare for the spout. After measuring the interior length of the tub spout and factoring in the dimension of the male adapter, I mark the proper tubing length.

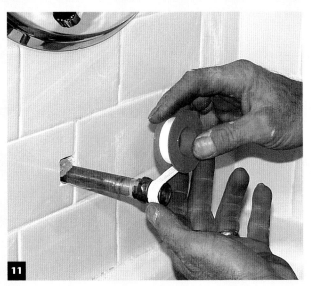

11

Don't forget the tape. I cut, clean, flux, and solder the male adapter onto the tubing. When it has cooled down, I wrap the threads with Teflon® tape.

8

Finishing up. To install the finish trim, I first slip the dome cover over the valve. To cover the holes on each side of the valve, I use what's known as a goof plate. After inserting the diverter control, I screw the goof plate onto the valve and attach the selector handle.

9

Not all goof plates are created equal. The large faceplates used to conceal holes in the shower wall are made to fit around specific valves. To avoid multiple trips to the plumbing supplier, check the fit of the valve cover plate and goof plate. While it's obvious that a Moen goof plate won't fit a Symmons cover, an aftermarket-brand goof plate meant for the same valve isn't a good fit, either.

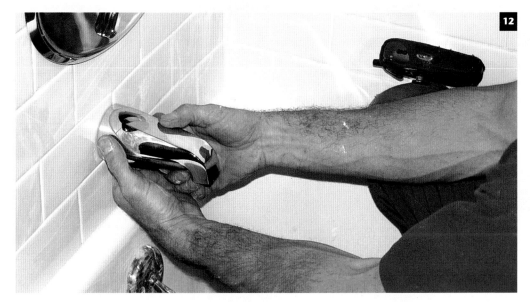

12

A good fit is snug against the wall. If I've measured correctly, the spout will thread onto the adapter and fit tightly against the tile.

Valve Replacement From the Front: How to Make the Best of a Tricky Tile Job

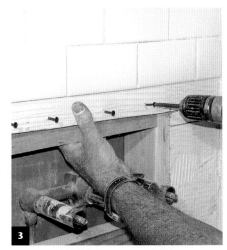

If I don't have access behind the shower and have to go through the tiled side of the wall, I call my favorite tile man, Tom Meehan. He has to remove and reinstall a small section of tile around the old valves so that I can install the new valve. Tom uses an angle grinder fitted with a diamond blade to cut a rectangle into the wall around the valves. A helper with a vacuum catches the dust (photo 1). He pulls out the section, removes a few more tiles (photo 2), and screws in a wood cleat at the top to catch the backerboard later (photo 3). Now I can remove the old plumbing and install the new valve (photo 4). When space is too cramped to use a heat shield, I spray combustible surfaces with a thermal shield gel. Sold under different brand names (Cold Shield™ and Hot Stop®), a 32-oz. bottle costs about $15.

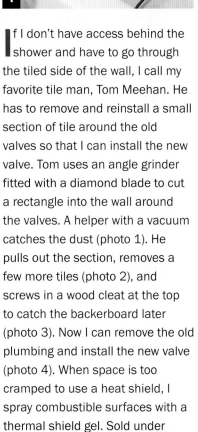

Install a Pedestal Sink

■ BY ED CUNHA

The only time my life as a plumber be-comes complicated is when my wife, the contractor, needs a job done on one of her projects. In these cases, I remember every husband's famous last words: "Yes, dear." One of her most recent projects was a powder-room remodel. An old vanity had been removed and the bathroom rearranged for more efficient use of space. A pedestal sink was the perfect space-saving solution for the washbasin. Installing one of these babies isn't rocket science, but there are a few tips and tricks that can make the job go more quickly and smoothly. Following the right installation sequence is key. Here's my take on demystifying the installation process.

Ed Cunha is a plumber who lives and works on Cape Cod, Massachusetts.

1. Plan for Visible Plumbing

A 2×8 let into the wall framing supports the anchor bolts that hold the sink. Remembering that the plumbing shows on a pedestal sink, put the supply pipes on the same horizontal line, equally spaced on each side of the waste line. Keep all rough plumbing at the manufacturer's recommended height and spread.

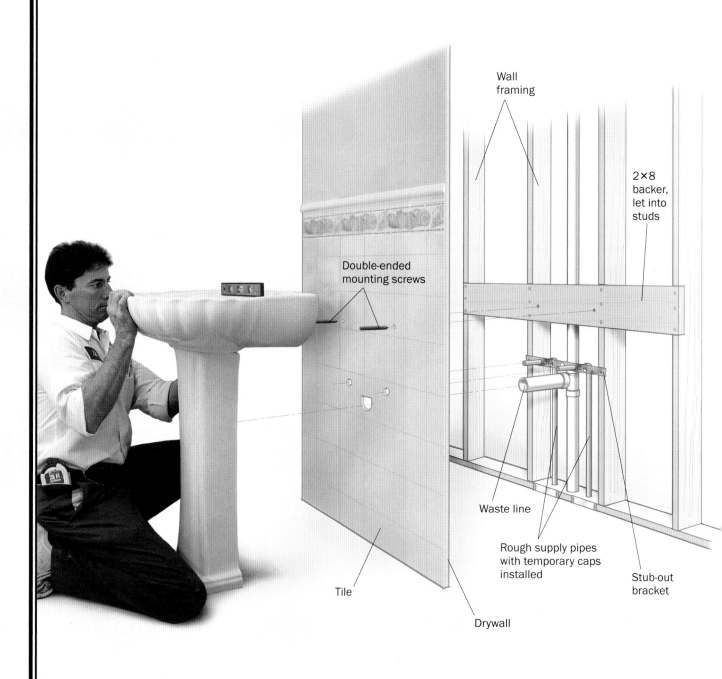

Wall framing

2×8 backer, let into studs

Double-ended mounting screws

Waste line

Rough supply pipes with temporary caps installed

Stub-out bracket

Tile

Drywall

Drilling Through Tile. Dry-fit the sink on its pedestal, checking its position with a level. **1.** Use a pencil to mark the position of the sink pedestal on the floor and the position of the bowl on the wall, then trace the mounting-bolt location onto the tile. **2.** Use a nailset or a common nail to nick the tile glaze to start the drill bit. **3.** Drill the hole with masonry bits, starting with a smaller bit and working up to the right diameter. **4.** Thread the double-ended mounting screws into place.

2. Supply Valves Go in Before the Sink

While the sink is still dry-fit, measure the distance between pedestal and wall to make sure there is plenty of space for the supply valves. Measure and cut the supply stubs so that the compression connection on the valve falls 3 in. from the wall (photo 1). Remember to slide the escutcheon onto the pipe before sweating the valve in place (photo 2). Before installing the sink, attach the faucet and the supply lines to it (photo 3). Smaller sinks can be held in your lap, and bigger sinks can be placed on the cardboard they were shipped in.

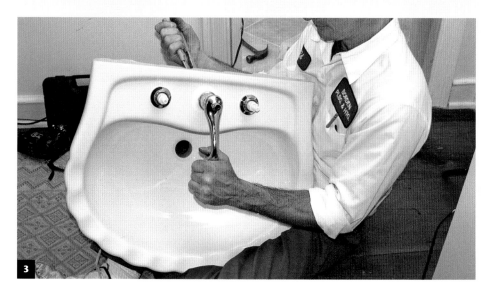

3. Hang the Sink

Slide the sink over the bolts (right), align the sink to the marks you made earlier, and snug the securing nuts. Connect the sink drops (sink supply lines) from the faucet to the valves (below). Flexible lines can be used, but solid lines look better for exposed plumbing.

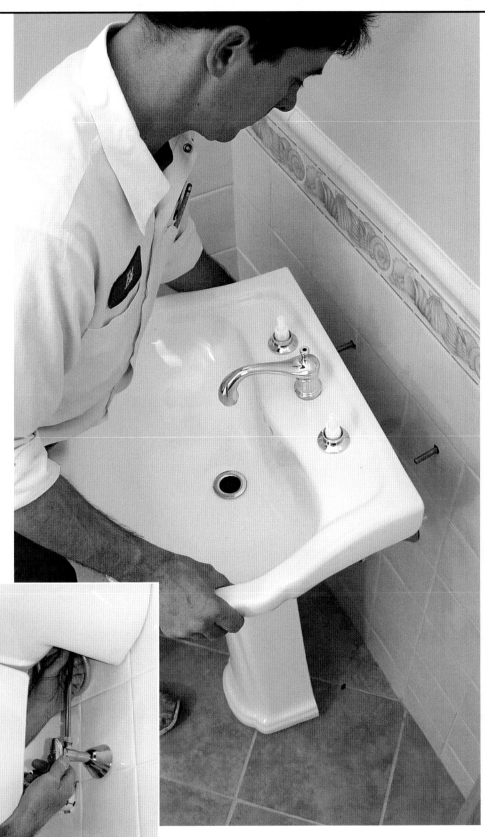

4. Then Hook Up

Mark the length of the drain line, then remove it and cut it to length (photo 1). Measure and cut the decorative chrome sleeve that fits over the white PVC drain (photo 2). The sleeve slips over the drain stub along with the escutcheon (photo 3), and the drain can be glued into place (photo 4).

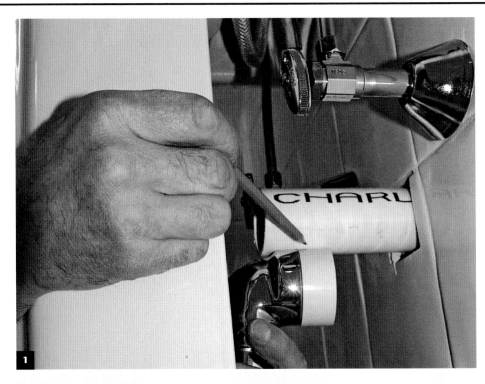

5. Drain and Done

It takes some creativity to use a wrench in the tight space behind the pedestal (below). The last step is inserting plastic shims from the hardware store to level the sink (bottom). It's now ready for action.

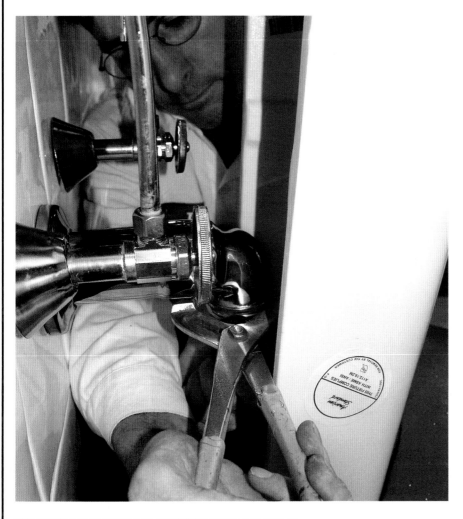

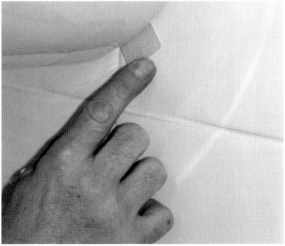

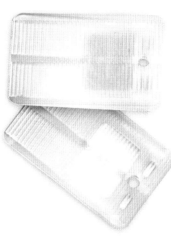

Don't Buy the Cheapest Sink

Pedestal sinks come in a wide variety of styles, and the price range is equally broad. Be wary of bargain models; many aren't cast well and can be difficult to install. Also, a poorly cast pedestal sink can have a high point in the basin or can be noticeably out of round.

Some plumbers have brands they like to install, but I prefer to look for specific features. The sink featured in the project on pp. 93–99, made by American Standard (www.americanstandard-us.com; 800-442-1902), had plenty of room underneath for anchoring the faucet. But the most helpful feature I look for in a pedestal sink is a base with a back that's wide open all the way to the floor. The open back gives you extra work area for easier trap installation.

Buyer's Guide: Toilets

■ BY NENA DONOVAN LEVINE

With so many factors to consider, picking the right toilet is no slam dunk. A buyer's first concern should be that it clears waste from the bowl without fail. But water conservation is a concern, too. Luckily, low-flush toilets offering great performance are relatively easy to find now, thanks to improved design and new flushing systems. Other features—price, aesthetics, the quietness of the toilet's flush, and ease of cleaning the fixture—depend on the user's priorities.

Nena Donovan Levine is a kitchen designer in West Hartford, Connecticut.

Why Buy a New Toilet?

- Toilets are by far the biggest water users in a household, consuming 30 percent to 40 percent of total volume.
- Residential 1.6-gpf (gallons per flush) toilets reduce water consumption by an average of 2 gpf compared to 1980s toilets; that's between 15,000 gal. and 20,000 gal. of water per year in a household of four.
- Replacing a 1.6-gpf fixture with a dual-flush toilet reduces water consumption by another 30 percent.
- High-efficiency toilets use 1.28 gpf, a 20 percent savings over today's standard toilets.
- Water conservation reduces the need for water-use restrictions and cuts down on the volume of wastewater requiring treatment. Government/water-company rebate programs can reduce the cost of a new toilet significantly.
- If every American home with older, inefficient toilets replaced them with WaterSense®-qualified toilets, it would save nearly 640 billion gal. of water annually, according to the EPA (see the sidebar on p. 107).

Flushing Systems Explained

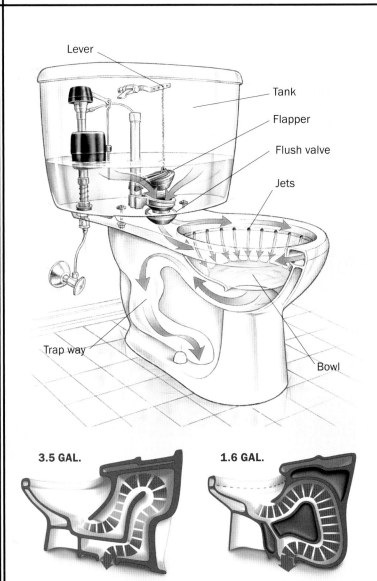

Lever

Tank

Flapper

Flush valve

Jets

Trap way

Bowl

3.5 GAL.

1.6 GAL.

Gravity-Fed

Most of today's toilets rely on the same technology that powered old-fashioned chain-pull toilets. These gravity-fed toilets must have the tank above the bowl to generate rushing water. Toilets designed to flush with 3.5 gal. had a deep bowl with a high, tight curve in the trap way (see the above left drawing). This constriction created plenty of siphoning power when more than 3 gal. of water rushed through the bowl. With just 1.6 gal., however, it became a choke point. American Standard's Champion 4® ($360; see the photo on p. 101) scores high marks for consistent clog-free performance, thanks to a wider trap way with minimal curves (see the above right drawing).

Pressure-Assist

A plastic tank within the toilet's porcelain tank holds water under air pressure to create a more forceful flush than gravity alone. These toilets stay cleaner than gravity-fed toilets because the water spot—the surface area of water in the bowl—is larger. They work well when older plumbing inhibits toilet performance.

Airtight inner reservoir

Pressurized water

More power, no sweat. The high-efficiency pressure-assist Mansfield® Eco-Quantum™ ($350) is condensation-free because of its tank-within-a-tank design.

Power-Assist

With an electric pump to move the water when the toilet is flushed, the tank can be below the bowl.

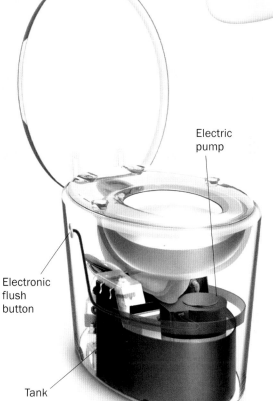

Electric pump

Electronic flush button

Tank

Where's the toilet? Kohler's Purist® Hatbox® ($2,700) is easy to mistake for a hamper. With an electronic flush and a self-closing seat, it's as quiet as a hamper, too.

Classic Two-Piece Toilet

Two-piece gravity-fed toilets often outperform one-piece gravity-fed commodes because the taller tank height generates more flushing force.

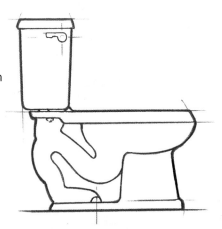

Easy-Cleaning Toilet

One-piece toilets are cast to create a single unit, a more difficult casting process that raises the price compared to two-piece toilets. Characterized by their low profile, the seamless tank and bowl simplify cleaning.

Toilet for Small Spaces

Wall-hung toilets work well in small bathrooms because the tank is in the wall. The sleek design makes for easy cleaning as well, especially of the floor.

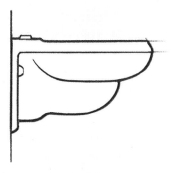

Bowl Shapes

Round bowls have a shorter, slightly wider profile, and elongated, oval-shaped bowls are several inches longer and slightly narrower.

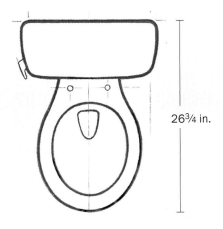

26¾ in.

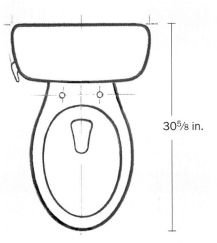

30⅝ in.

Dual-Flush Toilets Conserve More Water

Dual-flush toilets allow the user to choose the volume of water required to evacuate the bowl: 1.6 gpf for solid waste and 1 gpf or less for liquid or light waste. If all toilets in a four-person household are dual flush, water use per year should average 3,000 gal. to 4,000 gal. less than with 1.6-gpf models. This translates to additional savings and less wear and tear on a septic system.

Toto's gravity-fed Aquia® toilet (right) dispenses either 1.6 gpf or 0.9 gpf. All the flush water rushes down the bowl sides, which are steeply pitched. This washdown design helps clean and evacuate the bowl effectively. Sterling®, a Kohler company, also makes two gravity-fed dual-flush models that combine the wash-down capability of European toilets with the strong siphoning action of American toilets. American Standard emphasizes the role of the siphon in its recently introduced H2Option dual-flush toilets.

Other manufacturers of dual-flush toilets are Caroma®, Duravit, Villeroy & Boch®, and Vortens™.

Button one or button two? The Toto Aquia ($280) dual-flush toilet uses two flush volumes, 1.6 gal. or 0.9 gal. Users push the large button for a full flush and the small one for a water-conserving flush.

Personal Cleansing without the Paper

A decade ago at trade shows, this category barely had a toehold in the United States. Now manufacturers are tripping over themselves to unveil their latest bidet-action toilets. If water is the optimal way to clean our bodies, why not aim it at those parts that need frequent attention?

There's lukewarm enthusiasm in America for bidets, the separate fixture used for that very cleansing routine. They add expense in purchase and plumbing, and they require additional floor area in the bath. However, bidet seats, such as Bemis® Purité™, and the toilets with washing wands, such as Toto's Neorest® series, are a way to achieve the same results. These fixtures are in an estimated 60 percent of Japanese homes, and manufacturers hope they will find similar acceptance here. The elderly, postsurgery/postpartum patients, and individuals who cannot perform conventional toilet rituals are logical, not to mention grateful, users. More than a dozen companies making these toilets can be found at www.sanicare.com.

In most cases, installing one requires only a GFCI-protected outlet. Prices depend on the bells and whistles. At the low end of the price scale are retrofit seats such as the Purité ($700) or Brondell™ Swash™ 800 ($600). A full-feature personal-washing system with more aesthetic (and high-tech) appeal, like Toto's Neorest series, will take a bite out of your wallet; prices start at $1,800.

The lap of luxury. Toto invented the washlet (combination toilet and bidet) 40 years ago. Its top of the line, the Neorest 600 ($3,360), features washing wands with adjustable temperature spray, warm-air dryer, remote control, motion-activated seat and flush, dual flush, air cleaner, and heated seat.

EPA Label Signals
Savings and Performance

If you're looking for a toilet that saves water and removes waste effectively, you might consider one of the 430 models that bear the Environmental Protection Agency's WaterSense label. Toilets labeled under the program must use no more than 1.28 gpf (20 percent less water than the federal standard) and meet specific flush-performance requirements. WaterSense toilets can be found at all price points and use all types of flushing systems (in the case of dual-flush toilets, the flush volume is the average of one heavy and two light flushes). In addition to the water savings, many local utilities offer rebates on WaterSense-labeled toilets. For a list of those rebates, as well as more information on the program, visit www.epa.gov/watersense.

Waste not. Kohler's dual-flush Persuade® is among toilets that bear the EPA's WaterSense label.

Sources

American Standard
www.american-standard-us.com

Brondell
www.brondell.com

Caroma
www.caromausa.com

Duravit
www.duravit.com

Eljer®
www.eljer.com

Gerber®
www.gerberonline.com

Kohler
www.kohler.com

Mansfield
www.mansfieldplumbing.com

St. Thomas Creations®
www.stthomascreations.com

Toto
www.totousa.com

Villeroy & Boch
www.villeroy-boch.com

Vortens
www.vortens.com

Buyer's Guide: Bath Faucets

■ BY PATRICK McCOMBE

Most lavatory faucets are made from one of three materials: brass, zinc (pot metal), or plastic. Unlike cheap faucets, which have cast-zinc bodies, the most durable faucets have bodies and internal components made from machined and forged brass. Although concerns about lead in brass fixtures have resulted in the introduction of low-lead fixtures, brass construction remains a mark of quality. As a base material, it's less corrosive than zinc and more durable than plastic, which is often the base material in the least expensive faucets.

Weight is one of the best ways to measure a faucet's quality. High-quality brass faucets weigh noticeably more than those with internal components made of zinc or plastic. While you're handling the faucet, turn it over and look inside. If you can't tell by weight, it should be obvious when you look underneath whether the faucet is made of brass or zinc. Brass is dull yellow or reddish yellow, and zinc is dull gray or silver. If the faucet has plastic internal parts, that will be obvious, too. You can determine what metal the spout is made of by unscrewing the aerator and peeking inside.

While you're giving your prospective faucet a once-over, work the handles a few times. They should operate smoothly throughout their entire range of motion without a noticeable change in resistance. It's also a good idea to take a look at the drain assembly as the quality of these parts varies greatly. Once again, look for parts made of brass or stainless steel, and avoid flimsy plastic.

A Durable Finish

PVD isn't always pricey. The moderately priced Delta® Leland® has a stainless-steel PVD finish.

Burnished bronze. Kohler's Devonshire® is available with a bronze powder-coated finish and a lifetime warranty.

Chrome was introduced in the 1930s as a replacement for nickel, a soft metal that scratches easily. Chrome is still the most popular faucet finish; it's extremely durable, easy to clean, and inexpensive. In fact, it's often the base layer for other finishes, using a process called PVD, or physical vapor deposition. So-called brass, stainless-steel, and nickel finishes are not actual metal coatings but PVD finishes. Unlike powder-coated and painted finishes, the color in a PVD finish is retained on the molecular level, actually becoming part of the chrome. Manufacturers usually give PVD finishes a lifetime warranty and claim they're more durable than anything else. While PVD finishes are often found on high-end lavatory faucets costing hundreds of dollars, you may be able to find a faucet with a stainless-steel PVD finish for less than $140 at your local hardware store. Before the development of PVD, brass and finishes other than chrome often were protected by a clear lacquer coating that would break

down after a few years, which left an unattractive mottled appearance.

Over the past 10 years, so-called oil-rubbed bronze has emerged as one of the more popular finishes, especially for high-end bathrooms. There are two types of oil-rubbed bronze. Actual bronze, which has what manufacturers call a living finish, changes or develops a patina over time. The more common bronze finishes— variously described as aged bronze, antique bronze, blackened bronze, or brushed bronze, depending on the manufacturer—are really powder-coated finishes. Powder coatings are applied to a faucet with an electrostatic charge; then the faucet is baked in an oven until the finish molecules cross-link. This cross-linking is what gives powder-coated finishes their excellent durability. Powder coating is not as robust as PVD, however. Sara Maduscha, senior product manager for Kohler Global Faucets, recommends selecting bronze faucets and accessories with a lifetime finish warranty.

Long-Lasting Valves

Another consideration is the type of valves that control the flow of hot and cold water. Nowadays even moderately priced faucets are available with ceramic-disk valves, the most durable type, according to Kohler's Maduscha. Ceramic disks don't rely on soft rubber parts to control the flow of water. Instead, pairs of ceramic disks rotate against one another, turning the water on and off. When the holes in the two disks align, water flows through them; when they are rotated out of alignment, the water stops.

Ceramic-disk valves are a selling point, so faucet manufacturers generally advertise this feature on the product packaging—but not always. You can ask a salesperson if you're shopping at a kitchen-and-bath showroom, but it's best to write down the model number and contact the manufacturer or visit their website to confirm what's inside.

What about Ball and Cartridge Valves?

Ball, cartridge, and ceramic-disk valves have all but replaced the old compression-style valve for controlling water flow in modern faucets. Choosing a faucet with the best type of valve can ensure that it rarely, if ever, will need repair. Purchase a faucet wisely, though. Just because it's expensive doesn't mean it has the best valve. Style often trumps longevity.

Ball valves are most often found on faucets that have a single handle. When the hot- and cold-water supply lines are aligned with the holes in the hollow ball, water mixes and enters the faucet's spout. This valve has more moving parts than any other type of faucet valve, which means it's more prone to leakage and might require maintenance more often. Rubber seats, springs, and even the ball itself might need to be replaced over time.

Cartridge valves are composed of a hollow stem—which is connected to a water-supply line—that turns inside a metal or plastic sleeve. Both have a hole. When the faucet's handles are turned, the hole in the stem aligns with the hole in the sleeve to allow water to flow. Cartridge valves have few moving parts, so leakage points are minimized. Replacing an O-ring often solves leakage problems, but should the cartridge need replacement, you simply pull out the old cartridge and drop in a new one.

Spacing out. The wide spacing on the Cardiff from California Faucets® allows room to clean.

What's the Spread?

Compared to wall-mounted faucets, deck-mounted faucets don't take much head-scratching to position correctly. One thing you do need to check is whether the number of holes and the distance between the hot and cold taps on your sink—called the spread—matches that of the faucet you intend to buy.

The most common spread found on mass-produced vanity tops and pedestal sinks is 4 in. (called center-set). You also can find mini- and wide-spread faucets, some with spreads of 8 in. or more, that are more commonly used with stone and other custom vanities. Faucets that mount in a single hole are increasingly common because they take up a minimum of space, install easily, and are easy to clean.

Center-set faucets are generally made in one piece, and they're easy to install. However, the narrow space between the spout and the taps makes cleaning difficult. Wide-spread models usually have a pair of flexible supply lines that carry water from individual hot and cold taps to the spout, where it mixes. The wider space makes cleaning easier, but installation involves assembling more parts.

Here Is My Handle, Here Is My Spout

For regulating water flow, large lever handles are easier to operate than knobs, which is why they're required in commercial and institutional bathrooms by the Americans with Disabilities Act (ADA). Most people find levers easier to clean, too. Many faucets include an adjustable stop that limits hot-water temperature to prevent scalding—a good idea if you have small children or elderly family members in your home.

With designs that range from minimalist to gooseneck, it pays to consider how high you want the spout positioned over the drain. A height of 9 in. to 14 in. is best because it minimizes splashing, yet provides enough room for face washing. If you're likely to use the sink for more than just washing up—say, for bathing a baby or filling cleaning buckets—you might consider a faucet with a pullout spray.

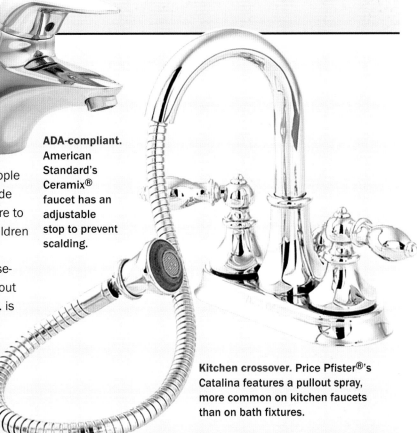

ADA-compliant. American Standard's Ceramix® faucet has an adjustable stop to prevent scalding.

Kitchen crossover. Price Pfister®'s Catalina features a pullout spray, more common on kitchen faucets than on bath fixtures.

Wall art. Kohler's Purist line includes both deck- and wall-mounted faucets.

Wall or Deck Mount?

The current fashion in high-end baths is the use of wall-mounted faucets. They not only look great, but they also stay cleaner than deck-mounted faucets because they're farther from the splashes of water, toothpaste, and soap common in busy bathrooms.

With a wall-mounted faucet, you need to figure out exactly where you want the spout in relation to the sink before the rough-in stage; changing your mind when the sink goes in will likely mean tearing into the wall. While there are no hard-and-fast rules, Kohler's Maduscha says most folks prefer to mount wall faucets 6 in. to 8 in. above the sink rim. You'll also need to know what tile or wall finish you're using; most standard faucet valves can accommodate up to 1 in. of total wall thickness, which limits tile thickness to about $\frac{1}{2}$ in. Thicker tiles and stone require different valves specially ordered from the manufacturer. Consider the dimensions of the sink when determining the length of the spout. It's best to keep the stream of water just short of the drain to minimize splashing and to provide enough room for washing.

Sources

American Standard
www.americanstandard-us.com

California Faucets®
www.calfaucets.com

Danze®
www.danze-online.com

Delta
www.deltafaucet.com

Grohe
www.groheamerica.com

Kohler
www.kohler.com

Moen®
www.moen.com

Price Pfister
www.pfisterfaucets.com

Faucets with a Conscience

Super saver. Moen's Icon faucet bears the EPA's WaterSense label.

WaterSense, a voluntary program of the U.S. Environmental Protection Agency, helps consumers to conserve water by identifying products that make better use of this precious resource. Traditional lavatory faucets spout about 2.2 gal. per minute (gpm) at maximum flow; models with the WaterSense label have a maximum flow of 1.5 gpm (at 60 lb. of water pressure). The standard also requires that WaterSense models deliver at least 0.8 gpm at 20 lb. of pressure, guaranteeing adequate performance even in homes that have very low water pressure.

Virtually all manufacturers now offer WaterSense-labeled lavatory faucets; a list of the hundreds of compliant products can be found on the Water-Sense website (epa.gov/water-sense). If you don't need a new faucet but want to save money and help the environment, WaterSense-approved replacement aerators are available for most faucets. You can even find aerators with flow rates as low as 0.5 gpm (www.niagaraconservation.com/aerators.html). The EPA estimates that installing one WaterSense faucet or aerator in an average household would conserve 500 gal. of water a year.

Against the flow. Aerators from Niagara Conservation® restrict maximum water flow from 2 gal. per minute (gpm) to 0.5 gpm.

Buyer's Guide: Bath Fans

■ BY JEFFERSON KOLLE

My father was cheap, or maybe he was just ahead of his time. During the 1970s energy crisis, when my brothers and I were teenagers and liked to take 20-minute showers, he'd pound on the door and say, "Hot water doesn't grow on trees. And turn on the fan in there," knowing that when one of us finally emerged, a hot, foggy mist would billow out and make the hall's walls glisten.

Then, 15 minutes later, he'd storm back upstairs, having heard the roar of the fan from the living room. He'd knock on the bedroom door, this time saying, "You left the fan on. Again." Seems like he wanted it both ways.

And today he could have had it. While he would have choked on the current gas prices, my father would have loved the bathroom-ventilation systems now available. Quieter motors and a variety of controls— including timers, motion detectors, and humidity sensors—work together as a set-it-and-forget-it appliance that even a grungy teen can't misuse.

Jefferson Kolle is a former editor at Fine Homebuilding.

Bath Fan Installation Tips

- Use duct mastic or foil tape to secure duct connections. Despite its name, don't use duct tape. It deteriorates over time.
- Insulate any fan ductwork that goes into an unheated attic. Otherwise, you risk water dripping out of the ceiling vent as hot, moist air from the shower condenses in the cold duct in the attic.
- Make sure any roof or sidewall wall vent has a screen to keep out critters. Also, if the dryer duct and the bath-fan duct look similar, prominently mark which is which. You don't want a screened dryer vent plugging up with lint and starting a fire.
- Ventilate all bath fans outside the house. Don't dump them into the attic, basement, or garage.
- Don't choose a fan that's too powerful, or you'll risk pulling all the air-conditioned or heated air out of the house.
- Check that the bathroom door has at least a ¾-in. clearance above the finished floor to allow proper entry of makeup air, as recommended by the Home Ventilating Institute (HVI).
- Connect a fan over a tub or shower to a branch circuit protected by a ground-fault circuit interrupter (GFCI).
- Don't exhaust a bath fan near a vented soffit, or next to a window or skylight, which can draw the moist air the fan has evacuated right back into the house.

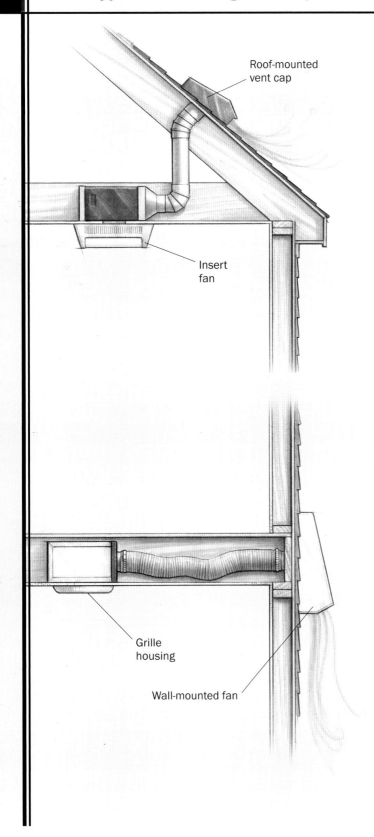

Roof-mounted vent cap

Insert fan

Grille housing

Wall-mounted fan

Panasonic FV-08VKML1
$220

Broan 757SN
$160

Ceiling Insert

A single fan with a housing that mounts between ceiling joists is called a ceiling insert. Panasonic's ENERGY STAR®–rated WhisperGreen® fans are available with compact-fluorescent bulbs (top left photo). Broan's® decorative models include metal trims in oil-rubbed brass, satin nickel (top right photo), or pewter. Ceiling-insert fans can be vented out the roof, as shown here, or out a sidewall.

Fantech PBW110
$160

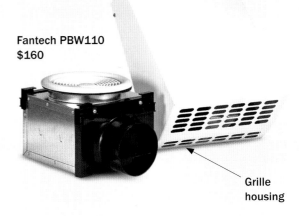

Grille housing

Wall-Mounted

If framing or accessibility constraints keep you from mounting a fan on the ceiling and venting it through the roof, consider a wall-mounted unit instead. This version by Fantech puts the fan and the motor outside, connected to a plenum called a grille housing.

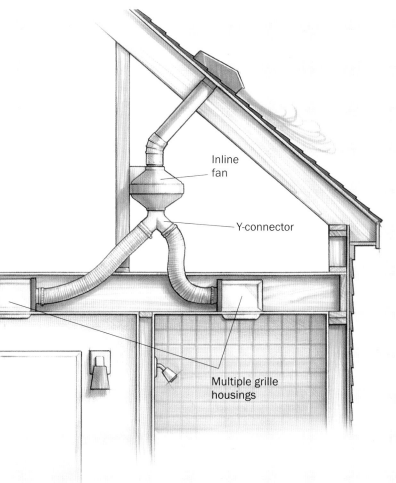

Inline
fan

Y-connector

Multiple grille
housings

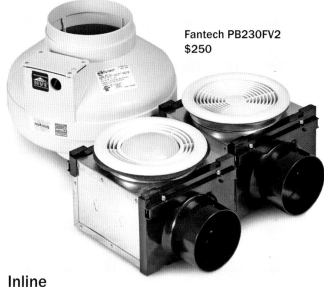

Fantech PB230FV2
$250

Inline

An alternative to mounting a fan on the bathroom ceiling is to install only the grille there and to locate the fan assembly in an attic or a crawl space. An inline fan can serve multiple grille housings in a large bathroom that has several moisture-producing fixtures. It also can be hooked up to ventilate multiple bathrooms.

Retrofit Kit

Some manufacturers sell quiet fans that replace their older, noisy ones. Once you determine the make and model number of your current bath fan, go to the manufacturer's website to see if a retrofit kit is available. Broan's model 690, which pulls 60 cfm, has a 3.0-sone rating; the company claims it reduces the sound of the original fan by 50 percent. The kit costs about $35, requires no new wiring or ductwork, and can be installed in 10 minutes, according to the company.

Broan 690 retrofit kit
$35

New Fans' Operation Is Whisper-Quiet

Roaring bathroom fans are a thing of the past. Fan noise is measured in sones, an indication of perceived loudness. A 1-sone sound compares to the sound made by a quiet refrigerator, while calm breathing is about 0.2 sones. The new fans from NuTone® and Panasonic are in the 0.3 to 0.4 range. In general, bigger fans make more noise than smaller ones, and larger ducts make less wind noise than smaller ones. Blow through a straw, then blow through a toilet-paper roll, and this is apparent.

Improvements in noise reduction have reached the upgrade market, too. If your fan makes a racket, several companies, including Broan, Fantech, and Continental Fan, sell quiet-fan retrofit kits that use existing housings and ductwork (see the sidebar on pp. 116–117).

What Type of Switch Is Right for My Bathroom?

Bathroom fans that are never turned on allow mold-inducing moisture to build up, and fans left on too long waste energy. Broan surmounts these problems with an adjustable behind-the-grille humidity sensor and timer that turn on the fan when moisture levels rise and shut it off after 5 minutes to 60 minutes.

One of Panasonic's WhisperGreen models has a built-in motion detector that keeps the fan going for 30 seconds to 60 minutes after it switches on. For better or worse, that means the fan turns on whenever someone enters the bathroom, whether to take a long, hot shower or just to get an aspirin.

For fans without onboard sensors, many companies, including fan manufacturers and electrical suppliers, sell wall switches with programmable timers (photos right).

The Leviton 6260M timer switch can be set to keep the fan on for 10, 20, 30, or 60 minutes and costs about **$25.**

Flip the Marktime® 42507 switch to the on position, and both the fan and the light will come on. If you flip it down to the timer position, the light will go off, but the fan will stay on to the user-set time of up to 60 minutes. The switch costs about **$35.**

The Lutron® MA-L3T251-WH is a combination dimmer/timer switch that can be adjusted for a 5-minute to 60-minute fan run-time; it costs about **$60.**

Sizing a Fan Isn't Always So Simple

The Home Ventilating Institute® (HVI) standardizes performance ratings for, among other products, bathroom fans. It also establishes guidelines for ventilation requirements, expressed as air changes per hour (ach), of different rooms in a house. Bathrooms require 8 ach. At the risk of abbreviation overload, you should know that the amount of air a fan can move is expressed in cubic feet per minute, or cfm.

HVI bath-fan sizing guidelines say that a fan should pull 1 cfm for every square foot of floor space in bathrooms up to 100 sq. ft. Above that, HVI recommends a ventilation rate based on the number and type of fixtures. For a toilet, shower, and tub, add 50 cfm each. For a jetted tub, add 100 cfm. In this example, you would need a 250-cfm fan.

That all sounds pretty straightforward, but these are under ideal, laboratory-grade conditions, which means the fan is hooked up to a short length of smooth-wall duct. In the real world, where ducts snake around obstacles and change material on their way to a distant roof cap, it gets more complicated.

Sizing a fan, then, can be more complex than relying on HVI's recommendation of 1 cfm per sq. ft. of floor area. The seemingly simple solution of just buying a bigger fan than what the floor-area calculations indicate you need also has pitfalls. Exhausting more air from a room than necessary sucks expensive conditioned air from your home and can pull in unconditioned air. In a relatively tight house, a fan that's too big can create negative pressure and suck flue gases from the chimney of the furnace or gas-fired water heater into the home.

Bottom line: If you have a complex duct run, consult a professional at a plumbing-supply house to determine the correct size of the fan you need.

PEX Water Pipe: Is Copper on the Way Out?

■ BY ANDY ENGEL

Most of us grew up in homes with copper pipes, and they were reliable enough that we gave them little thought. Joining them takes soldering skills so simple that my father taught me when I was about 10. But a relative newcomer, PEX, is mounting a serious challenge to copper plumbing, despite the latter's long history of reliability.

PEX is a clumsy acronym for cross-linked polyethylene, meaning that it's a strong plastic suitable for potable water. Popularized as the go-to product for radiant-floor heating, PEX has seen its use for potable water grow by about 40 percent annually. This isn't happening on a lark. The scuttlebutt among plumbers is that PEX is every bit as reliable as copper, yet costs less and is faster to install.

My own experience with PEX involves two underfloor heating systems. The plastic pulls through holes in joists and studs with slightly more difficulty than Romex®. Fittings for PEX are expensive, but you don't use many.

What Is PEX Anyway?

Polyethylene is a common plastic whose inert nature makes it valuable for food containers (or in this case, potable-water pipes). You likely poured milk into your morning coffee from a polyethylene jug. PEX differs from your milk jug in that it's cross-linked—its molecules are rearranged to resemble a chain-link fence—which greatly increases the plastic's strength.

Although the polyethylene PEX is made of comes from oil, it is one of the more environmentally friendly plastics. No pipe is without environmental cost. Although much of the copper used for pipe is recycled, all of it originally came from mines. And the manufacture of another plastic pipe, CPVC (chlorinated polyvinyl chloride), is said to release dioxin, a potent carcinogen.

Cross-linked polyethylene, although chemically the same as the milk jug, is much tougher and has a "shape memory," allowing it to be stretched or kinked and return to its original shape with time or heat. PEX's shape memory is so strong that at least two

No soldering required. Rolls of plastic tubing are far easier to snake through joist and stud bays than are lengths of rigid copper pipe. For this reason, PEX is an excellent choice for remodeling and retrofit situations, allowing you to snake plumbing lines almost as easily as you can snake wire. PEX has a much better resistance to bursting when frozen than copper, and is far less expensive, about 50¢ per ft. vs. 85¢ per ft. for copper, with far fewer fittings to buy.

PEX Isn't Copper's First Plastic Challenger

Copper tubing appeared in the early 1920s, was tested and standardized by the American Society of Testing and Materials (ASTM Standard B88) in 1932, and owned a significant market share by the 1940s. Copper was the newcomer taking on industry giants lead pipe, which appeared in A.D. 79, and galvanized-steel pipe, which appeared toward the end of the 19th century. By 1994, more than a billion feet of copper pipe was being used in houses every year. That's eight times around the earth, or about 80 percent of the market.

The other 20 percent was made up of a new generation of challengers: plastics. Plastic water pipes called chlorinated polyvinyl chloride (CPVC), cross-linked polyethylene (PEX), and polybutylene (PB) were introduced to the European and North American markets beginning in the 1960s. Of these pipes, polybutylene gained ground the quickest. After its introduction in 1978, PB pipe was installed in about 6 million houses, but after 10 years to 15 years, it began to fail and disappeared from the mainstream housing market around 1995.

CPVC is a reasonable alternative with a 40-year track record but few compelling reasons to switch from copper. It costs about the same, and after the PB debacle, plumbers have been gun-shy of plastics. CPVC has 10 percent to 15 percent of the residential plumbing market, but with copper's price skyrocketing, CPVC could gobble up a larger share—if not for the less-expensive and easier-to-install PEX.

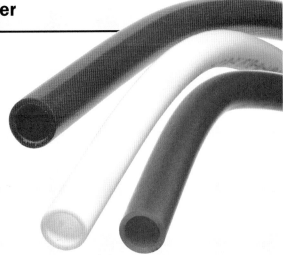

You don't have to use red for hot. But you can. The different colors make it easier to keep track of which tubes are hot and cold. That can be handy for homeowners.

`'A CPVC 4120 HI TEMP 100 PSI @ 180°F -690 KPA`

CPVC is reliable but rigid. This plastic pipe is less expensive than PEX but more time-consuming to install.

CPVC

Specialized fittings are a boon to remodelers, allowing copper, PEX, and even CPVC to share the workload. Compression fittings are one of many non-crimping systems available (this one is from Zurn®). Also available for PEX are threaded fittings with national pipe thread, which can combine with threaded pipe and threaded pipe fittings.

PEX

A reusable slip-in fitting uses stainless-steel teeth inside the collet to lock the tubing in place (SeaTech®). An internal O-ring makes the seal. To remove, push in the collet while pulling out the tube.

Collet

Tough Tubing, Tougher Connection. These sections of tubing were put to the tests, both tensile and compression. In both cases, the connection held fast. The tube at top was stretched from 4 in. to 11 in. under 400 lb. without tearing the pipe or breaking the connection (high-tensile tubing test). While the tubing at left eventually did burst, it took almost 1000 psi to do it (compression check). Water pressure in most homes runs about 50 psi.

manufacturers, Rehau® and Uponor, rely on it to create leakproof joints, rather than on crimped metal fittings.

Three different processes are used for cross-linking this plastic, and the resulting products are called PEXa, PEXb, and PEXc. The original, PEXa, dates from the 1950s and has been sold in Europe for radiant-floor heating since 1971. Rehau's Lance MacNevin says PEXa is more forgiving than either PEXb or PEXc, claiming that it can be stretched to about 400 percent of its manufactured length before failure. But even PEXb and PEXc can stretch substantially. Because of PEXc's cross-linking process (cross-linked with a laser beam while lying flat), it tends to stay flat when rolled out. If you've ever found yourself being followed by a coil

of pipe when installing an underground plastic water line, you'll appreciate this seemingly small advantage. PEXb and PEXc are somewhat less expensive than PEXa.

Copper Has a Long Track Record and Few Drawbacks

The American Society of Testing and Materials (ASTM) standard governing copper pipe and fitting sizes was implemented in 1932. That means you can buy a fitting at the hardware store today that will slide right onto a 75-year-old copper pipe.

Studies have shown that copper has anti-microbial properties, perhaps helping keep

Copper

Special fittings allow you to connect copper and PEX in various ways, depending on your needs.

Buying PEX online

Many manufacturers deal only with licensed plumbers, but online stores sell to anyone. Here are some of our readers' favorite sites:

- www.mvsupply.biz
- www.houseneeds.com
- www.pexsupply.com
- www.blueridgecompany.com
- www.pexconnection.com

A Leakproof Joint Made Faster Than Soldering

There are many systems for crimping PEX joints. Some are available only to licensed plumbers, but online stores (see "Buying PEX online" on p. 123) will sell to anyone. The Zurn system (shown here) is fast and easy.

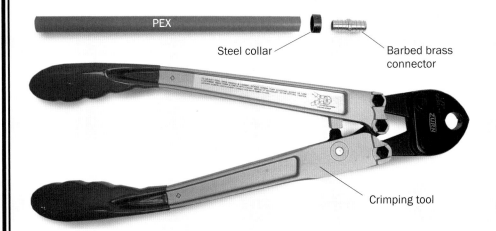

PEX

Steel collar

Barbed brass connector

Crimping tool

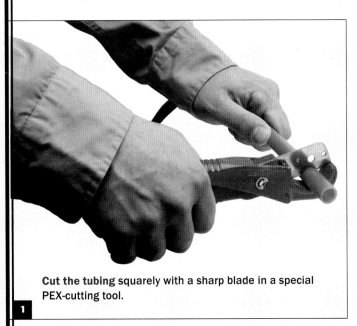

Cut the tubing squarely with a sharp blade in a special PEX-cutting tool.

1

Slip a steel collar over the tube, then insert a barbed brass connector into the tube.

2

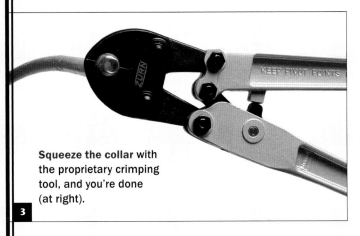

Squeeze the collar with the proprietary crimping tool, and you're done (at right).

3

4

your water safe to drink. About the only functional downside to copper is that it is susceptible to developing pinholes in areas with corrosive acidic well water. Andy Kireta Jr. of the Copper Development Association agrees that corrosion can happen, but he notes that "because we have historical data that indicate the areas prone to acidic water, we know to recommend conditioning to neutralize the water's pH in these places." Kireta also points out that "copper tube is one of only a handful of materials that can be recycled and maintain the same level of purity as the original product. That is, you can melt down old copper pipe and use it to make new copper pipe. Most recycled materials, such as steel, paper, and plastics, drop a notch in quality each time they're recycled."

The last plastic pipe to make serious inroads into copper's market dominance was polybutylene, a flexible gray tubing that had problems with leaky fittings. Blame and lawsuits flew like snow in a New England blizzard, and polybutylene disappeared from the market in the mid-1990s. CPVC is approved for domestic potable water, but it doesn't have a huge market share.

If Copper Worked and Plastic Failed, Then Why Risk Using PEX?

With many plumbers concerned about plastic pipe after the polybutylene debacle, why take a chance on the PEX generation? First, PEX isn't polybutylene. Polybutylene failed for a number of reasons, one of which was that the fittings were made of a type of plastic that didn't react well with the chlorine used by many municipal water-treatment facilities.

All approved PEX tubing meets ASTM standards. Pipe intended for potable water must meet additional National Sanitation Foundation (NSF) and American National Standards Institute (ANSI) rules.

To ensure compliance, samples are tested annually, and unannounced audits of PEX manufacturing plants are made three times a year.

Second, PEX often performs better than copper: It isn't susceptible to pinhole leaks because it's chemically inert; it won't clog with mineral scale because its inner surface is smoother; and it has superior resistance to bursting from frozen water. Jim Bolduck, a Cumberland, Maine, plumber, told me about a PEX-plumbed house he'd seen that had lost its heat in the dead of winter. "That house froze so solid that the boiler split open," said Bolduck. "All the PEX survived, though."

Dana Bres, a research engineer with HUD's Partnership for Advanced Technology in Housing (PATH), points out another asset: "Quality control for all types of plumbing tube (PEX, copper, and CPVC) is excellent, so the pipes themselves rarely leak. Leaks happen at joints, and copper plumbing is loaded with joints. PEX comes in rolls hundreds of feet long, which minimizes the number of joints and the potential for leaks." In 2004, PATH listed PEX plumbing systems using plastic distribution manifolds as one of the top-10 emerging technologies.

PEX and Copper Can Combine for Remodeling

Like CPVC, PEX comes in the same outside diameters as rigid copper pipe (nominal diameter plus ⅛ in.). At least one manufacturer, WattsRadiant™, makes compression fittings that work with all three types of pipe. In fact, in my own house, I needed an emergency repair fitting after drilling a hole through a PEX heating line. The old-time plumbing store I went to didn't carry PEX fittings, but they did sell me a compression coupling for copper pipe. That was five years ago, and although it's not a code- or manufacturer-approved joint, it doesn't leak, either.

Flexible Pipe Also Offers Design Flexibility

Incorporating manifolds into the layout can save water and energy because you eliminate most of the pipe between the water heater and the faucet. Although blue (cold water) lines are shown in these layout examples, hot-water layout would be similar.

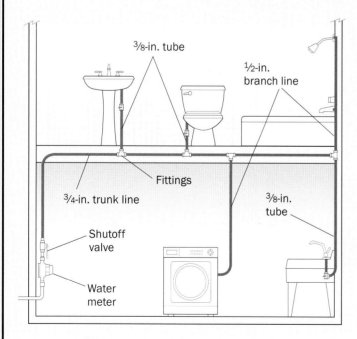

3⁄8-in. tube

1⁄2-in. branch line

Fittings

3⁄4-in. trunk line

3⁄8-in. tube

Shutoff valve

Water meter

Trunk-and-Branch Systems

Easy, but they waste a lot of water. Traditional systems consist of large-diameter (usually 3⁄4 in.) trunk lines to distribute water throughout a house. Smaller branch lines (1⁄2 in. and 3⁄8 in.) tee off to feed individual fixtures. Trunk-and-branch systems have several disadvantages, notably a large number of fittings, which are costlier, slower to install, and more likely to leak than is a single run of pipe. Also, a lot of water goes down the drain before hot water reaches the faucet.

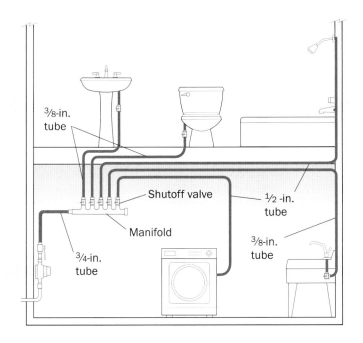

3/8-in. tube

Shutoff valve

Manifold

1/2-in. tube

3/8-in. tube

3/4-in. tube

Home-Run Manifold Systems

Use the least hot water and the most pipe.
A large-diameter (3/4 in.) main water line feeds the manifold; smaller lines run from the manifold to each fixture. Any fixture in the house can be shut off at the manifold. And because home-run systems don't rely on a large pipe for distribution, you save both water and energy. Simply put, you don't have to leave the faucet running as long before hot water reaches the sink. This design flexibility has a cost, however. Because a dedicated line is going to each fixture, you use a lot of PEX and drill a lot of holes.

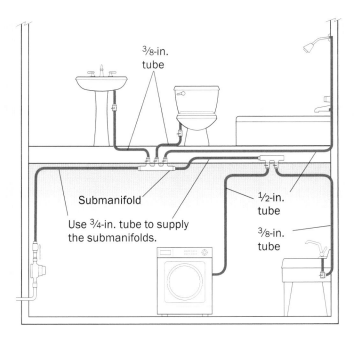

3/8-in. tube

Submanifold

Use 3/4-in. tube to supply the submanifolds.

1/2-in. tube

3/8-in. tube

Submanifold Systems

Can be designed to save hot water. There are many ways to design submanifold systems, which require far less pipe and drilling than a home-run system. Rather than one main manifold, each bathroom, laundry, and kitchen gets its own submanifold. The simplest system, pictured here, won't save any water over a trunk-and-branch system, but other submanifold systems can be configured as water and energy savers by incorporating a main manifold and a recirculating pump.

For blended systems, PEX manufacturers have fittings that join to PEX at one end and either solder to copper or glue to CPVC on the other. Additional fittings allow PEX to terminate and stub out of the wall or floor.

PEX Can Be Run Like Copper, but That Won't Maximize Its Potential

You can configure PEX plumbing systems several ways, and it's possible to do so in ways that save water. PEX can be configured like a traditional copper system, with larger-diameter trunk lines teeing off to smaller branch lines that feed individual fixtures. Doing so will eliminate some elbows and their potential leaks, but it doesn't take best advantage of PEX's properties.

The PEX industry pushes several other configurations, all of which start out at a plastic or copper manifold, where the hot and cold mains split off to various parts of the house (see the photo below). With manifold systems, each branch has its own shut-off valve, analogous to an electrical system's circuit-breaker panel. Using PEX with manifolds can save water and energy because hot water reaches remote sinks more quickly.

National Plumbing Codes Treat Copper and PEX Equally

Because PEX and copper are the same outside diameter, one might wonder how the inside diameters compare. After all, inside diameter determines flow rate. The walls of PEX pipe are thicker, so the inside diameter is smaller. For several reasons, however, all U.S. plumbing codes treat copper and PEX interchangeably when considering adequate water flow. The inside of PEX is smoother than copper, and PEX offers fewer flow restrictions because it is bent into sweeping curves instead of turning with sharp elbows the way copper and CPVC do.

Although PEX has been part of national plumbing codes since the early 1990s, not every jurisdiction has adopted those codes. Before using PEX for potable water, check with your local building inspector.

Normal PEX Isn't UV-Tolerant

One major shortcoming is that left unprotected, PEX deteriorates when exposed to the sun's UV-rays. Copper doesn't have this problem. Most PEX is warranted for only 30 days of direct sun exposure, but some premium lines coated with a UV-inhibitor are good outside for a year. Even the best PEX can't be left exposed outside, so copper must be used for pipe that's to be exposed to the elements. If you're using PEX under a slab, either cover the pipe where it stubs out of the concrete, or spend more for PEX with a UV-inhibitor.

PEX also is susceptible to damage from certain oil- or solvent-based compounds, and can allow these compounds to pass

PEX doesn't have to be messy. Although some plumbers complain that **PEX** installations are messy, others enjoy the drama of the final hookup to the manifolds. Red (hot) and blue (cold) tubing can make a confusing mass of pipe understandable.

through the pipe and into the water. Never bury PEX (even if coated with a UV-inhibitor) in contaminated soil, and avoid oils and greases when working with PEX.

How Do I Persuade My Plumber to Use PEX?

I've spoken to a number of plumbers about PEX and didn't find one who flat out refused to use it. Most plumbers who've used it were enthusiastic. Those who were reluctant fell into two camps. A common concern was voiced by Dave Trone, a plumber in Columbia, New Jersey: "Plastic and brass expand at different rates, and I think that leaks where PEX pipe joins to brass fittings are simply a matter of time." The other concern I heard surprised me. "It just doesn't look as neat as copper," said one Nebraska plumber.

Although it's true that joints between PEX and brass don't have copper's 75-year track record and that leaking polybutylene fittings are still a sore spot with some plumbers, a representative from Zurn Industries addressed Trone's concerns: "PEX is the most engineered and tested plumbing material out there. Its shape memory allows it to expand and return to size repeatedly, so we're confident of the long-term viability of the joints." Then he showed me a PEX-brass connection that had been subjected to 990 pounds per square inch (psi) pressure. The joint had held tight, but the PEX tube burst. Residential water systems generally run at less than 50 psi.

When I brought up the Nebraska plumber's complaint about neatness with Rehau's MacNevin, he replied, "We hear that occasionally. That's why we also make PEX in 20-ft. rigid lengths that can be used in visible locations like a basement."

Manufacturers seem concerned that leaks caused by poor workmanship could undermine the acceptance of PEX, so many offer on-site training and certification to licensed plumbers. In fact, many of the biggest play-ers, such as Rehau and Uponor, won't sell their product to uncertified installers. But because PEX and its fittings are sold through plumbing-supply houses, enforcement of this mandate is spotty. Other manufacturers, however, believe their systems are so simple to use that they're sold at major home centers. PEX and its fittings are also readily available online (see "Buying PEX online" on p. 123).

If your plumber still isn't buying into PEX, bring up labor savings. Says Bres: "In a recent PATH field evaluation of otherwise identical homes, it appears that using PEX shaves a day off the plumbing installation, reducing the install time from three days to two."

When I plumbed my new house in 1999, I ran PEX for the radiant-floor heat. For the potable-water system, though, I reflexively used copper because conventionally that's how you plumb a house. I had a good time soldering the joints and figuring out the system. Being a competent but slow do-it-yourself plumber, I needed about a month's worth of weekends to do the job.

If I had my house to plumb over again, I'd configure PEX in a submanifold system. I think that approach offers the best bang for the buck, and it makes good use of PEX's advantages. Because I'd want to do the work myself, several of the best systems on the market that require pro installation would immediately be out of contention. So my choices would be limited to materials I could buy online or locally. Given that, I wouldn't shop for a particular brand. All the PEX manufacturers I spoke with left me feeling comfortable with their products. I'd look for a supplier of a system—that is, I'd want the fittings and the pipe to come from one manufacturer. I'd look for a supplier happy to provide advice and support. And I'd expect the job to take about half the time.

Andy Engel is the editor of Professional Deck Builder *and he's also a former editor at* Fine Homebuilding. *He lives in Roxbury, Connecticut.*

Preventing Moisture Problems in Bathrooms

■ BY MARY JO PETERSON

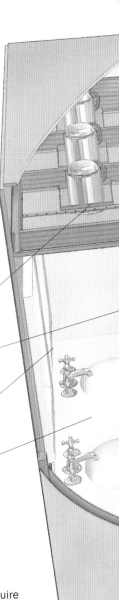

As a veteran kitchen and bath designer, I've created my share of glamorous bathrooms, complete with oversize showers, giant soaking tubs, whirlpools, saunas, and the like. I wish I could say that all of my clients come to me for the bathroom of their dreams; sadly, a lot of them show up at my door after water leaks and humidity have rendered the bath of their dreams unusable. Today's bathrooms unleash copious amounts of moisture, all of which must be carefully controlled, or the results can be devastating (can you say *mold*?).

Although I'm glad to have the business, I want my work to last, so I'm always alert to improvements in products, design, and construction that address these issues. Following are a few of the strategies that I use to ensure that none of my dream baths ever become someone else's nightmare.

Recessed lights belong inside conditioned airspace. **4**

Vulnerable tub joint gets two layers of caulk. **5**

Coved countertop contains water. **6**

Penetrations into unconditioned spaces are sealed with foam.

THE BATH OF YOUR DREAMS SHOULD NOT BECOME A NIGHTMARE
Complicated bathrooms require careful design, but as long as moisture control is accounted for during every step in the process, even the most ambitious creation can expect many years of useful service.

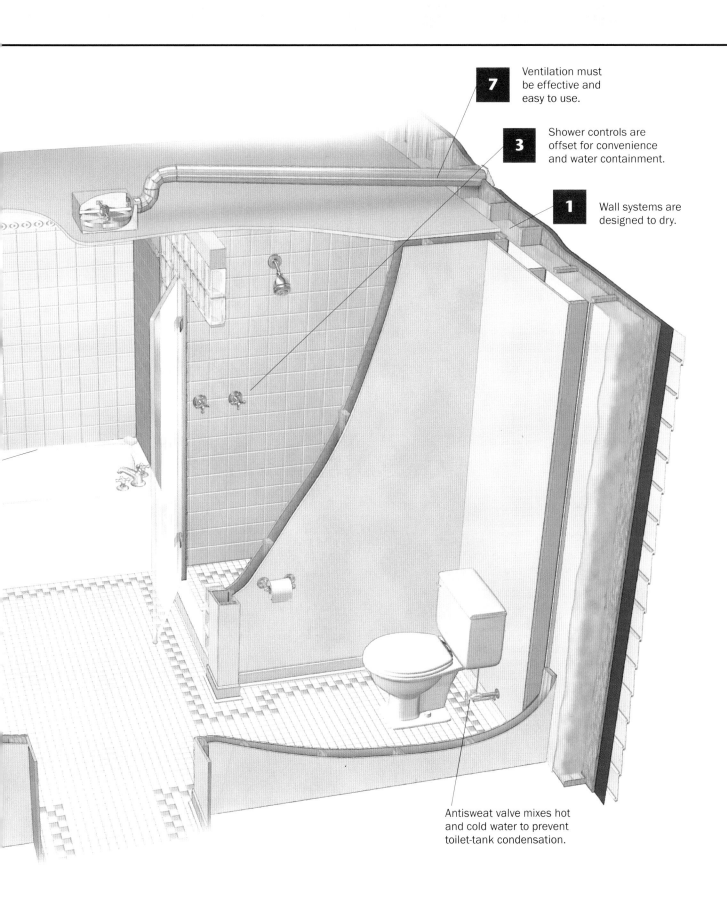

7 Ventilation must be effective and easy to use.

3 Shower controls are offset for convenience and water containment.

1 Wall systems are designed to dry.

Antisweat valve mixes hot and cold water to prevent toilet-tank condensation.

1 Exterior Bathroom Walls Must Be Able to Dry

COLD-CLIMATE WALL ASSEMBLY DRIES TO THE EXTERIOR

In regions where interior humidity levels are typically greater than those on the outside, a vapor barrier is placed on the interior surface of the wall, while permeable sheathings are used on the exterior.

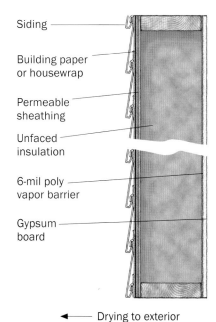

Siding

Building paper or housewrap

Permeable sheathing

Unfaced insulation

6-mil poly vapor barrier

Gypsum board

◄──── Drying to exterior

HOT/HUMID-CLIMATE WALL SHOULD DRY TO THE INTERIOR

In regions where exterior humidity levels are typically greater than those on the inside, the vapor barrier goes on the outside of the wall, while permeable sheathings go on the inside.

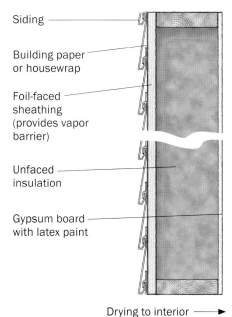

Siding

Building paper or housewrap

Foil-faced sheathing (provides vapor barrier)

Unfaced insulation

Gypsum board with latex paint

Drying to interior ────►

PLUMBING LINES BELONG INDOORS

If plumbing lines have to be located along exterior walls, the best way to maintain an impermeable vapor barrier (and to ensure that the pipes won't freeze) is to frame a nonstructural "water" wall for pipes inside the exterior wall.

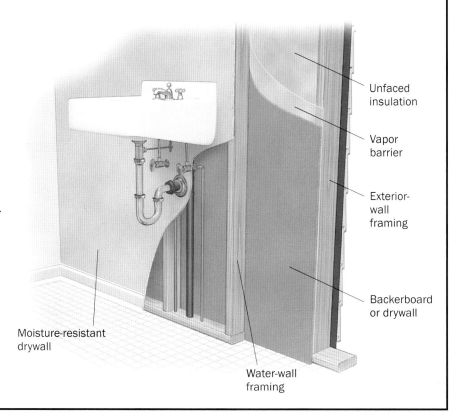

Moisture-resistant drywall

Water-wall framing

Unfaced insulation

Vapor barrier

Exterior-wall framing

Backerboard or drywall

Use the Proper Wall Assembly for the Climate

Today's tight construction methods yield big dividends in terms of comfort and energy efficiency, but they don't dry out like the drafty walls of old. To prevent trapped moisture, exterior bathroom walls must be designed carefully. In certain climates, a properly installed vapor barrier can be a valuable part of that design.

Assuming all other aspects of moisture control are handled correctly, the main influence on the location of the vapor barrier is climate. Moisture tends to migrate from areas of greater (or warmer) concentrations into areas of lesser (or colder) concentrations. In a heating climate, such as New England where I work, a vapor barrier is placed on the interior of wood-frame walls and ceilings, and permeable exterior sheathings are installed to allow any moisture that gets into the wall cavity to dry to the exterior (see the sidebar on the facing page). In a cooling climate, however, the opposite might be true. Wall assemblies in general and vapor barriers in particular are controversial subjects. Consult a building-science expert in your area to find out what might work best for you.

Leave No Draft Unsealed

Because most moisture that enters framing cavities is airborne, air leaks present significant opportunities for moisture to build up behind walls or under floors. Common spots for drafts include rough-ins for electrical, plumbing, or mechanical systems; drains for tubs and showers; and cutouts for recessed lights. My policy is that any penetrations in the floor, wall, or ceiling must be sealed with polyurethane foam, silicone sealant, or some other appropriate material. My subcontrac-

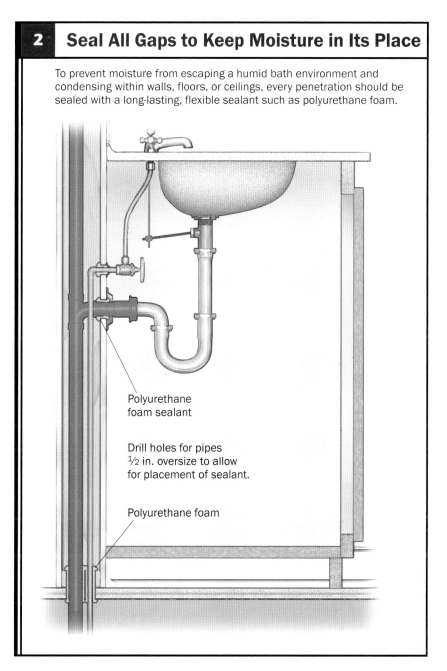

2 Seal All Gaps to Keep Moisture in Its Place

To prevent moisture from escaping a humid bath environment and condensing within walls, floors, or ceilings, every penetration should be sealed with a long-lasting, flexible sealant such as polyurethane foam.

Polyurethane foam sealant

Drill holes for pipes
½ in. oversize to allow
for placement of sealant.

Polyurethane foam

tors make sure that any holes they cut in the subfloor are large enough to allow for at least ¼-in. thickness of flexible sealant around the pipes (see the sidebar above).

Recessed lighting presents another draft problem. Conventional fixtures are way too porous for use in a bathroom. To avoid filling the space above with moisture, recessed fixtures located in insulated ceilings must be airtight and carry the IC-rating, which indicates that they are designed to be covered

Looks Funky but Makes Sense

Placing water controls closer to the door (rather than centered on the showerhead) makes them easier to use and lessens the likelihood of water escaping from the shower.

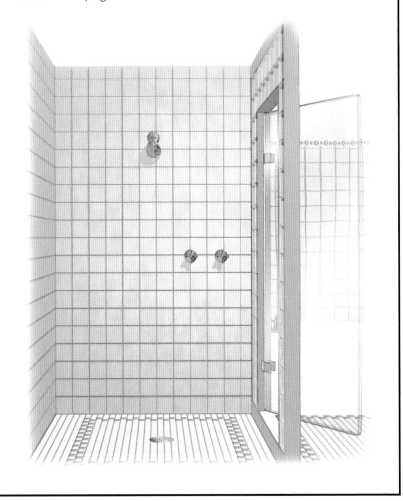

never be located along exterior walls. Unfortunately, I don't always have a choice.

Having done my first bath designs on the Connecticut shoreline—where winter winds off Long Island Sound can freeze pipes in short order—I would never take the risk of placing plumbing pipes within exterior walls. If I were stuck with an exterior-wall location, I would frame a second wall for pipes just inside the exterior wall that would provide room for proper insulation and for the creation of a healthy wall system (see the sidebar on p. 132).

In addition to the placement of the shower, the location of the shower fixtures can have a big impact on moisture control. I like to offset the water controls closer to the shower door to make them easy to reach without opening the door all the way (see the sidebar at left). I also try to make sure that the showerhead is not easily directed at the door opening.

Glass doors provide better water containment than shower curtains, but access can be a problem. Shower curtains can be weighted to hold them to the floor for better water containment. Another simple solution for keeping water inside a curtained shower is to fashion a dam in each corner using a bead of silicone placed at a diagonal.

with insulation. A better solution is to place recessed lights within soffits or dropped ceilings. From my designer's standpoint, a well-framed soffit creates interesting sightlines and avoids any penetration into unheated spaces (see the sidebar on the facing page).

Locate Showers and Tubs on Interior Walls, If Possible

The best solutions from a designer's standpoint don't always agree with those of a building scientist. These experts tell me, for example, that tubs and showers should

One-Piece Tub Enclosures Are Boring but Leakproof

When it comes to the materials to be used for a tub (or shower) enclosure, there are almost no limits as to what is available: tile, glass block, solid surface, cultured marble, plastic laminate, acrylic, and gel-coated fiberglass, to name a few. If I listened only to building scientists, the choice would be clear: one-piece tub units. As long as the drain is installed properly, the framing is correct, and the floor is supported adequately, experts tell me that the chance that one of these units will ever leak is minuscule.

4 Keep Recessed Lights inside Conditioned Airspace

Although recessed lights that carry an IC-rating can be placed in an insulated ceiling, an airtight installation is extremely difficult to achieve. A better solution (if ceiling height permits) is to install these lights inside a soffit or a dropped ceiling.

Covering walls and ceilings with drywall before building the soffit creates an air barrier between conditioned and unconditioned spaces.

Drywall

Ceiling joist

Drywall

Wall studs

Most of my clients want more pizzazz, and most of the time they choose tile. Unlike one-piece shower surrounds, tile is not impermeable to moisture—largely because of the grout. In my experience, however, as long as tile is installed properly over a cement board substrate, a tile enclosure will be fine (see "Sources," on p. 139). Applying tile directly over the moisture-resistant gypsum (greenboard) is asking for trouble.

Solid-surface materials such as Corian® also require a proper substrate, but they eliminate the need for maintaining grout. Glass block is a good choice for a custom shower because it's less permeable to moisture than is tile. Glass block is also available in many shapes and textures and includes structure and finish in one complete package.

Accessories and built-ins for custom showers also must be designed carefully. Soap and shampoo cubbies must not compromise the water or vapor barriers, so I never design these niches to be set into an exterior wall. I also make sure that the horizontal surfaces of cubbies as well as shower seats are sloped to shed water back into the shower.

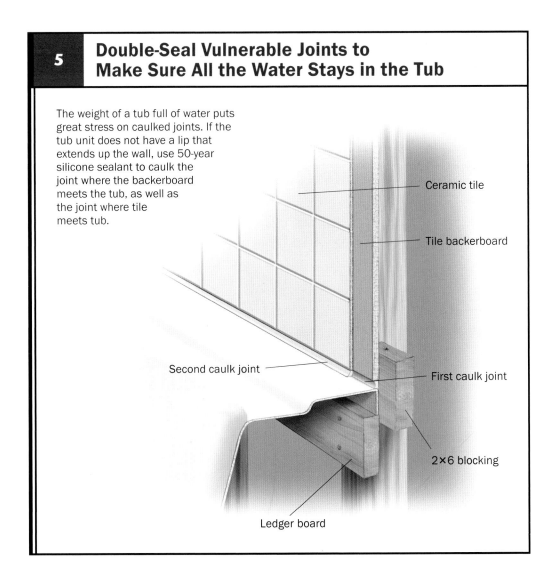

The weight of a tub full of water puts great stress on caulked joints. If the tub unit does not have a lip that extends up the wall, use 50-year silicone sealant to caulk the joint where the backerboard meets the tub, as well as the joint where tile meets tub.

Ceramic tile

Tile backerboard

First caulk joint

2×6 blocking

Ledger board

Second caulk joint

Tubs and Whirlpools Require Flexible Sealant

Stand-alone tubs generally have fewer moisture problems than do showers because they contain water better. The weight of that water can be a problem, however, as can frequent splashing, such as children like to do.

The constant filling and emptying of a tub demands flexible seams where the sidewalls meet the tub. My installer uses only the highest-quality silicone sealant. In addition to caulking the joint where tile meets tub, he caulks the joint between the backerboard and the tub (see the sidebar above).

Wall surfaces surrounding a whirlpool tub that doesn't get heavy use simply can

be painted greenboard. Whirlpools release a lot of steam, however, so if I know that the client has big plans for the appliance, I insist on the same type of wall assembly I'd use for a shower.

Integral Countertops Make Trouble-Free Vanities

Undermount lavatories are popular these days because they offer clean lines and easy cleanup. Their only drawback, however, is a vulnerable seam that's hidden beneath the countertop. For clients who don't mind poking their heads under the sink a couple of times a year, this seam is not a problem. Some clients want their baths to be as maintenance-free as possible, however. For them, I recommend an integral basin/countertop made from a seamless material such as cultured stone. Integral countertops can be ordered with or without a seamless backsplash. Occasionally, the client requests a tile backsplash to be installed over an integral countertop; in these cases, I specify that the countertop be formed with a ½-in.-tall cove on which the tile will rest (see the sidebar at right). The cove eliminates the seam against the wall where water can collect and eventually escape.

Don't Sweat about the Toilet

The plumbers that I use add extra blocking around the toilet's drain line to stiffen the subfloor. This practice helps ensure that the wax ring seal will never be broken. Properly installed toilets don't leak, but they might sweat. Condensation on the toilet tank typically occurs during the summer months when the water in the tank might be 20°F or even 30°F cooler than the air. This seemingly harmless occurrence can result in some serious problems: Moisture drips onto the floor and seeps beneath the floor covering, and eventually, the subfloor starts to rot.

Air-conditioning is one way to prevent condensation; if that's not an option, you can retrofit an existing toilet with a prefabricated toilet-tank insulation kit, or install an antisweat valve in the water-supply line. (An antisweat valve adds a small amount of hot water to the toilet's water supply. Adjustable models can regulate the hot-water supply during the months when it's not needed.)

If purchasing a new toilet, consider one with factory-installed tank insulation or a pressure-assist system that stores water in a pressurized plastic tank within the porcelain tank.

6 A Little Bit of Lip Keeps Water in Its Place

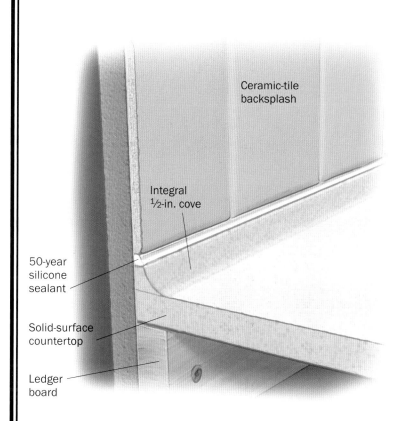

Ceramic-tile backsplash

Integral ½-in. cove

50-year silicone sealant

Solid-surface countertop

Ledger board

A solid-surface vanity top that combines basin, counter, and backsplash in one seamless unit is leak-proof but creatively limiting. Substituting a ½-in. tall cove for a full backsplash still contains water splashes yet allows clients to trim the vanity top with a variety of materials, such as tile or mirrors.

An Open Window Is Not a Ventilation System

Toys such as steam showers, whirlpools, and soaking tubs dump huge amounts of moisture into the air. Even a perfectly designed bathroom will suffer if it doesn't have an adequate ventilation system. While some codes still consider an operable window sufficient ventilation, that's asking for trouble, as is trying to get by with a cheap, noisy fan. On every one of my bath designs, I specify a high-quality, ultra-quiet fan that's correctly sized to the space (see the sidebar on p. 139).

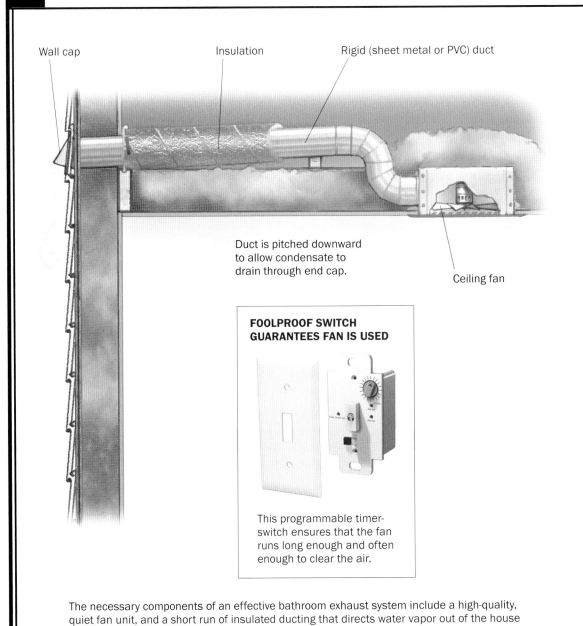

Wall cap

Insulation

Rigid (sheet metal or PVC) duct

Duct is pitched downward
to allow condensate to
drain through end cap.

Ceiling fan

**FOOLPROOF SWITCH
GUARANTEES FAN IS USED**

This programmable timer-
switch ensures that the fan
runs long enough and often
enough to clear the air.

The necessary components of an effective bathroom exhaust system include a high-quality, quiet fan unit, and a short run of insulated ducting that directs water vapor out of the house before it's able to condense.

Fixtures as Well as Room Dimensions Determine Which Fan Unit Is Necessary

Exhaust systems are rated in cubic feet per minute (cfm) of air moved, and the National Kitchen and Bath Association (NKBA) offers a formula as a starting point for calculating the minimum ventilation needed for a bathroom: cubic feet of the room × 8 (air exchanges per hour) ÷ 60 (minutes) = required cfm rating.

Another easy guide is to figure 1 cfm per sq. ft. in bathrooms that are smaller than 100 sq. ft.; in bathrooms that are larger than 100 sq. ft., allow 50 cfm per standard fixture (shower, tub, toilet, steam shower), plus 100 cfm per hot tub.

Oversize bathrooms can benefit from multiple intake points connected to one remote fan. Typical locations of exhaust inlets are near moisture sources, such as the whirlpool, shower, or steam shower and toilet area, as well as near closet or storage areas that might be exposed to moisture. With this type of system, it is important to check the cfm at each location.

The installation of a ventilation system is critical. The duct system should take the shortest, most direct route to the outside; but even a short run of ductwork can be troublesome. To prevent trapped condensation, I use insulated, rigid pipe, and I make sure that the pipe has a slight pitch, either to the outside or back to the fan (see the sidebar on the facing page).

In tight, modern houses, an adequate supply of return air must be provided in conjunction with the ventilation. This can be as simple as making sure there is at least an inch of airspace under the entry door or as complicated as providing a passive make-up-air duct.

Even if it's perfectly installed, an exhaust system won't get the job done unless it is used. I strongly recommend to my clients that they leave the fan running—with the door closed to make sure moisture cannot escape into neighboring rooms—for at least 30 minutes after taking a shower or using a whirlpool. Placing the ventilation fan on a timer makes following this advice easy. An even easier solution is to connect the fan to a humidistat that will automatically turn the fan on and off according to the humidity levels.

Baths Need Regular Maintenance

After eliminating unnecessary moisture problems, constant vigilance is the key to maintaining a dry bathroom. Indoor air humidity and temperature must be controlled throughout the home. What might be a comfortable condition for the homeowner might not be ideal for the home. Relative humidity between 40 percent (winter, generally) and 65 percent (summer), with a constant temperature around 68°F, is best. Frequently inspect visible caulk joints and redo them when they first show signs of degrading. At least a few times a year, get a good flashlight and summon the courage to poke around in the basement, crawl spaces, and attic, looking for any signs of moisture leaks, musty odors, or nasty bugs.

Mary Jo Peterson, is president of Mary Jo Peterson, Inc., a Connecticut-based design firm that focuses on residential projects and provides design support to major homebuilders and product manufacturers nationwide.

Sources

Dow Corning®
989-496-6000
www.dowcorning.com
Silicone sealant #795

Dupont®
800-426-7426
www.dupont.com
Solid-surface countertops

Georgia-Pacific®
800-284-5347
www.gp.com
Denshield tile backerboard

James Hardie® Building Products
888-542-7343
www.jameshardie.com
Hardibacker tile backerboard

Panasonic
866-292-7292
www.panasonic.com/Building ventilation fans

Precision Plumbing Products Inc.
503-256-4010
www.pppinc.net
Antisweat valve kits

Tamarack Technologies
800-222-5932
www. tamtech.com
Timer switches, humidistats

USG Corporation
800-874-4968
www.usg.com
Durock® tile backerboard

A Sloping Floor for a Barrier-Free Bath

■ BY TOM MEEHAN

One aspect of civilization that the Romans got right was the tiled bath. Since then, Europeans have built tiled bathrooms that present no distinction between the shower and the rest of the room. This design's success depends on lots of tile and a mortar substrate that slopes to a strategically placed floor drain. A lack of thresholds also makes this kind of bathroom perfect for wheelchair access.

On this side of the pond, so-called Euro-baths have found their way into the mainstream of American bathroom design, even when accessibility is not a factor. I recently completed such a bathroom for a homeowner who needed an accessible, elegant design (see the photo on the facing page).

Reframing the Floor around the Drain Gets You Ahead of the Game

The key to a successful Euro-bath is pitching the floor to a single drain in or near the shower area. The best way to create this pitched floor is with a full mortar bed, also called a mud job. The process is similar to what is done for a shower-stall floor, only now the mud job covers the entire room.

Before taking on a bathroom of this type, I check the existing floor for level. A floor pitched strongly away from the drain is usually enough for me to pass on the job. I also make sure the floor is good and strong without any bounce.

Showers without borders. Tumbled slate, custom accent tiles, and a built-in shower seat add up to a stylish open bath that's also wheelchair-accessible.

A Contour Map Identifies Flat and Sloping Sections

With an open plan and more than 100 sq. ft. of floor area, this bathroom can accommodate both level and sloping sections of floor. Located well away from the shower, the tub and the toilet can sit on level floors. The contour lines show how the mud layer slopes to the shower drain. The pitch is about ¼ in. per ft. in perimeter areas and slightly steeper in the shower area. A slight downward slope near the doorway drops the transition height to equal the adjacent floor while letting the rest of the bathroom drain to the shower.

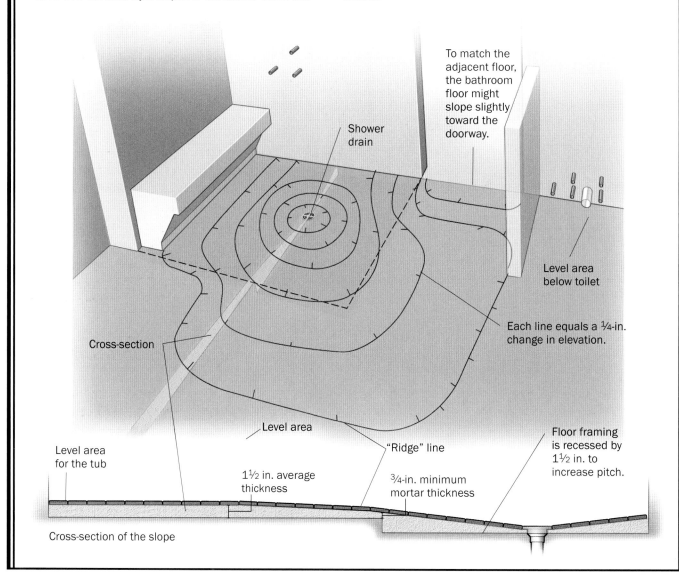

To match the adjacent floor, the bathroom floor might slope slightly toward the doorway.

Shower drain

Cross-section

Level area below toilet

Each line equals a ¼-in. change in elevation.

Level area

"Ridge" line

Floor framing is recessed by 1½ in. to increase pitch.

Level area for the tub

1½ in. average thickness

¾-in. minimum mortar thickness

Cross-section of the slope

To keep the finished floor from ending too high at doorways, I had the carpenters on this job frame a 1½-in. recess in the shower area, replacing the 2×10 joists with narrower 2×6s that then were tripled for added strength. When reframing isn't a viable option (on an upper floor or a slab, for instance), I get the drain as low as I can and use a smoother tile (2×2 or less) that won't impede the flow toward the drain. I also have the option of using NobleFlex® drain flashing (see "Alternative Membrane and Drain Flashing" on p. 147). When the reframing was complete, I put a layer of #15 felt paper over the entire floor, then nailed down 2½-lb. diamond-mesh galvanized-wire lath with 1½-in. roofing nails, overlapping the mesh joints by at least an inch. Felt paper isolates

Get a Head Start on the Slope

To increase the floor's pitch toward the drain over a short distance, the floor framing is recessed by 1½ in.

Narrower joists are tripled for extra strength.

A layer of #15 felt paper creates a barrier so that the moisture won't seep out of the mortar. To give the mortar purchase on the floor, I nail a layer of 2½-lb. diamond-mesh galvanized-wire lath over the paper with galvanized roofing nails. The mesh seams should overlap about 1 in.

the mortar bed from movement in the subfloor and keeps the wooden subfloor from sucking moisture out of the mortar as it dries. The wire lath anchors the mortar to the floor.

Screeds Guide the Floor Pitch

In a large mortar box, I mix the mortar by thoroughly combining 25 shovelfuls of sand to each bag of portland cement; then I add water a little at a time (about 5 gal. per batch) until the mortar has a dry but stiff consistency. It should stay together when you form it into a ball in your hand. I plan for about 35 sq. ft. of coverage averaging a 1½-in. depth with each batch mixed as above.

I set the drain low enough to get a pitch of at least ¼ in. per ft. (see the drawing on the facing page). After gluing the drain flange to the PVC waste line, I dump buckets of mortar around the perimeter of the room and around the drain in 8-in.- to 10-in.-high mounds. Using a slightly wetter mortar mix, I make sure to fill the space under the flange completely.

The height of the door threshold where the bathroom floor meets the adjacent floor is the most critical juncture. Taking into account the thickness of the floor tile and the height of the adjacent floor, I pack and flatten the mortar with a steel trowel until it is the proper height. With that as a standard height, I then work my way around the room's perimeter. Because water is unlikely to reach the far corners of the room, I level the perimeter of the floor to allow the toilet, the vanity, and the tub to sit squarely.

The Shower Is a Big Shallow Bowl

Now I'm ready to pitch the floor of the shower area. I dump a few buckets of mortar between the level perimeter and the drain, and pack the mortar into that area.

So that the mortar screeds evenly, one end of the straightedge rides on the perimeter while the other end rides on the drain. As I work, I switch tools constantly, screeding with a level, packing with a steel trowel, and smoothing the surface with a wood float.

I find it easier to scrape the surface down to the finished height, so I keep the mortar slightly high, and use trowels and levels to pitch the floor to the drain. I continue to check the slant of the floor, pulling the excess mortar toward me to create a shallow bowl in the shower area.

Once the bowl is formed, the mortar is smoothed with a wood float to take out any small high or low spots. Finally, I use a steel trowel at a shallow angle to press in a tight, shiny finish.

A Membrane Waterproofs the Mud

Because mortar is porous, it needs to be water-proofed with an impervious membrane. The membrane needs not only to cover the floor but also to extend at least 6 in. up the wall.

I used Schlüter's Kerdi membrane (see "Sources" on p. 149 and "A Layered Membrane Seals the Mortar" on p. 146). Any nonlatex-modified thinset (also known as dry set) will attach the membrane to the

Begin with Mounds of Mortar

A dry mix of mortar is distributed evenly around the perimeter of the room.

After cementing the drain at the proper height, I fill the space below the flange with a slightly wetter mortar mix, making sure the space is filled completely. I then distribute more mortar around the shower area.

Pack, Screed, Smooth

My basic strategy here is to bed the drain, pack the mud flat, and level around the higher perimeter of the floor, and then work at creating the slope between high and low.

I use a short level and a long aluminum straightedge to get the perimeter level.

A wooden float held at a 45-degree angle pushes the mortar tight against the wall.

Levels of different lengths also serve as screeds, enabling me to check the pitch of the floor while removing bumps and filling hollows.

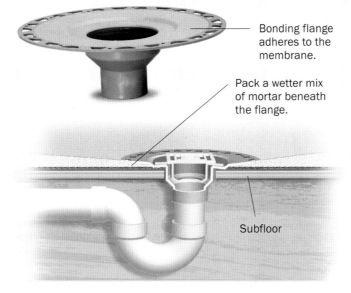

Bonding flange adheres to the membrane.

Pack a wetter mix of mortar beneath the flange.

Subfloor

As I pack and fair the slope of the mud, I use a wooden float to remove high spots and a steel trowel held at a low angle to finish the surface.

A Layered Membrane Seals the Mortar

To waterproof the mortar bed completely, the membrane is applied in sequence.

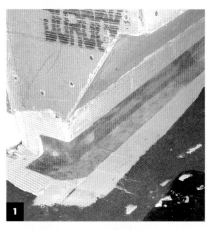

The inside- and outside-corner pieces are applied; any excess thin-set is squeezed out and removed.

A 5-in.-wide strip is folded into the seam where the floor meets the wall and is cemented in place.

After dry-fitting the first large sheet of membrane, I roll it up, then trowel thinset onto the sheet's place on the floor. A wide taping knife pushes the excess thinset to the edges and from around the drain. Successive sections should overlap by about 3 in.; I leave about ½ in. of space where the wall and floor membranes overlap the corners (see the drawing above).

Alternative Membrane and Drain Flashing

Many manufacturers make waterproofing membranes, but over the past 25 years, I've used two brands with great success: Schlüter and Noble (see "Sources" on p. 149). Although the membranes are slightly different, they both yield the same great results. Both manufacturers also offer reliable technical support.

For this project, I used Schlüter's Kerdi membrane. The equivalent Noble product is NobleSeal® TS. I usually opt for the Kerdi because it's thinner (8 mil versus 31.5 mil for the NobleSeal TS) and therefore easier to work. Many installers choose NobleSeal TS, however, precisely because it's thicker and heavier.

Both products are covered with a thin layer of fabric on each side that lets them adhere to thinset. However, Schlüter specifies that Kerdi be installed with nonlatex-modified thinset (dry set), while Noble requires a latex-modified thinset. One major advantage to NobleSeal TS is that it acts as a crack-isolation membrane in addition to waterproofing, making it an excellent choice over substrates like wood that are likely to move over time.

NobleSeal TS comes in 5-ft.-wide rolls, while Kerdi comes in 5-in., 7¼-in., 10-in., and 39-in. widths. Kerdi makes preformed inside and outside corners; NobleSeal TS has just outside corners.

For the project featured here, I used Schlüter's drain system, Kerdi-Drain. Noble makes an interesting product called Noble-Flex drain flashing (see the drawing at right)

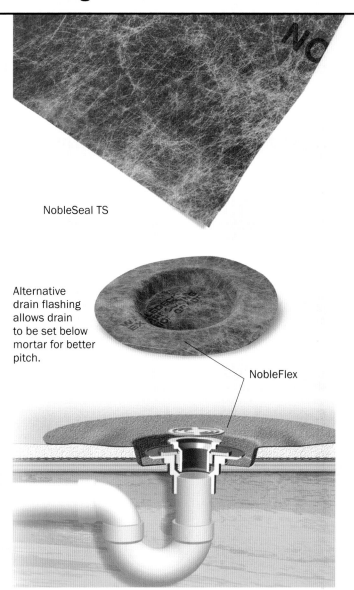

NobleSeal TS

Alternative drain flashing allows drain to be set below mortar for better pitch.

NobleFlex

that can be used with most drains that have clamping rings. Resembling an upside-down hat, this flashing fits between 16-in. on-center joists, enabling me to gain a lot of floor pitch without reframing the floor.

Tiling Is the Easy Part

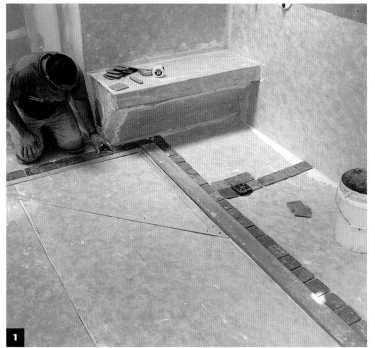

With a straightedge and a large folding square, I set the layout dry using a snapped chalkline to keep the irregular stone tile straight.

I embed a three-piece adjustable drain in thinset.

I use a few taps of the trowel handle to set the finished flange to the level of the tile. The rest of the floor is tiled a few rows at a time. After the tile is installed, the stone is sealed, grouted, and sealed again to complete the floor.

mortar bed, but I used the recommended DitraSet (see "Sources" at right).

I begin by spreading thinset along the edges of the mortar bed and walls with a ³/₁₆-in. V-notch trowel, then press the Kerdi preformed inside and outside corners into place. Using a taping knife with rounded corners, I squeeze out excess thinset from beneath the corners, then coat the exposed surfaces to attach the overlapping layer.

Next, I cut a length from a 5-in.-wide roll of membrane and fold it in half down the middle. Pressed into the corners, the membrane should cover each side by 2½ in. and overlap the previously installed corner pieces. As before, I flatten the membrane and squeeze out excess thinset.

Before installing the larger sections of membrane over the mortar bed, I sweep the floor thoroughly. Beginning in the shower area, I cut to length all sections and dry-fit them. The first section goes over the shower drain; I carefully mark and cut out the drain location, using a manufacturer's template.

I also use a permanent marker to draw a line onto the mortar at the edge of the first section to guide the thinset application. Each successive section overlaps the line of the previous section about 3 in. After each section is dry-fit, I roll it up, number it, and put it aside.

When all the sections are cut, I spread thinset to the first guideline with a notched trowel. Spreading the thinset in one direction, I extend it onto the flange of the drain, then slowly unroll the first membrane section, keeping the edge aligned with the guideline. As membrane is unrolled, I press it into the thinset with a taping knife, keeping the membrane straight and flat by continually pushing excess thinset to the edge of the section. After bedding each section, I spread the thinset to the overlap line of the previous section before repeating the process. Finally, I apply a floor-to-ceiling membrane to the shower walls, using the same method that I used on the floors to ensure a waterproof installation.

Smaller Tile Means Better Drainage

After the membrane sits overnight, the floor is ready for tile. I protect the membrane with felt paper or cardboard to minimize any puncture risk. The only difference from a regular tile installation is that the membrane is now the substrate for the tile.

On this job, I installed 4-in.-sq. tumbled slate on the floor. Larger tile requires a little more pitch because the tiles can't conform to the shape of the floor as well as smaller tiles. I gave this floor a little more pitch than I would for a typical handicapped-accessible bath because of the unevenness of the slate, which also can impede drainage.

I always start with a dry layout to see where the tile courses land. I try to use full tiles in areas that are seen first and most frequently. For this project, I first measured eight courses off the wall and snapped a chalkline across the room. Then I used a large folding square from C.H. Hanson® (see "Sources" at right) to establish a line perpendicular to the first line. I dry-fit tiles along both lines and adjust the layout as needed. In this case, I was able to get the 4-in.-sq. drain to land perfectly within the tile layout.

With the layout set, I spread thinset and install tile the same as I would for any similar installation, working about 15 sq. ft. at a time. No matter what product is used, always follow the manufacturer's recommendations. Again, I used DitraSet to set the tile. Because the uneven surface of the tile makes it harder to clean, I gave the tile two coats of sealer before grouting and another sealer coat afterward.

Tom Meehan is a second-generation tile installer who has been installing tile for more than 35 years. Tom lives with his wife, Lane, and their four sons in Harwich, Massachusetts, where they own Cape Cod Tileworks.

Sources

Bostik®
800-7BOSTIK
www.bostik-us.com
DitraSet thin-set

C.H. Hanson Tool Co.
800-827-3398
www.chhanson.com

Noble Company
800-878-5788
www.noblecompany.com
NobleFlex and
NobleSeal TS

Schlüter Company
800-472-4588
www.schluter.com
Kerdi system and
Kerdi drain

Upgrading to a Tile Shower

■ BY TOM MEEHAN

When fiberglass shower units were first introduced in the 1970s, they were the stars of the plumbing world. Inexpensive and relatively easy to install, they didn't crack and were easy to clean. Fiberglass units had their own problems, but they worked.

These days, bathrooms are a big renovation target for many homeowners, who might not know how to deal with their old fiberglass tub/shower units (see the photo below). For this project, I removed the old tub unit in pieces, did a little carpentry, and

Work from the top down. The first cuts are made in the corners to separate the unit's walls from the tub.

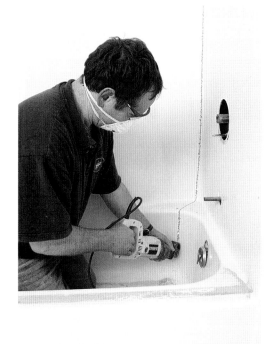

TIP

Avoid floods, shocks, and breakage. When cutting, watch out for pipes and wires, and check in neighboring rooms for items like mirrors or vases that might vibrate and fall onto the floor.

It takes only a few cuts. Once the walls are removed, the tub should come out in pieces that are small enough to cart away without scratching walls and woodwork (below).

Time to call a plumber. The plumber levels the drain (left) so that it matches the shower-pan floor. He also replaces the mixing valve with a thermostatic pressure-balanced shower valve (right).

had a plumber relocate the drain and mixing valve. After that, the job was like any other: a site-built pan, backerboard substrate, and tile (in this case limestone) combined with some interesting details that made a luxurious shower (see the right photo on p. 150).

Demolition: The Fun Stage with Quick Results

To take out the existing shower unit, I first shut off the main water valve to the house, then start disassembling the plumbing fixtures (mixing valve and showerhead, etc.).

The door is closed and the fan turned on to keep dust out of the house. I always cut the drywall along the outside edge of the unit with a knife, hammer, and chisel to avoid damaging the drywall outside the shower stall.

Next, I put on a dust mask and safety glasses, stick a new wood-cutting blade in a reciprocating saw, and start cutting from the top, working down (see the top left photo on p. 151). It helps to have someone hold some of the loose pieces, which vibrate as they are cut free from the rest of the unit.

Each piece that's carted away makes it easier to attack the remaining section; usually the unit comes out in five or six pieces.

Securing the backer-board. The author likes to nail the substrate every 6 in. to 8 in. (see the photo at far left). All seams are then sealed with fiber-glass-mesh tape bedded in thinset and troweled smooth (see the photo at left).

Don't Forget to Change the Vent Location

Plumbing code requires that a specific distance between the vent and the trap be maintained, based on local codes. Check with the local building inspector before starting.

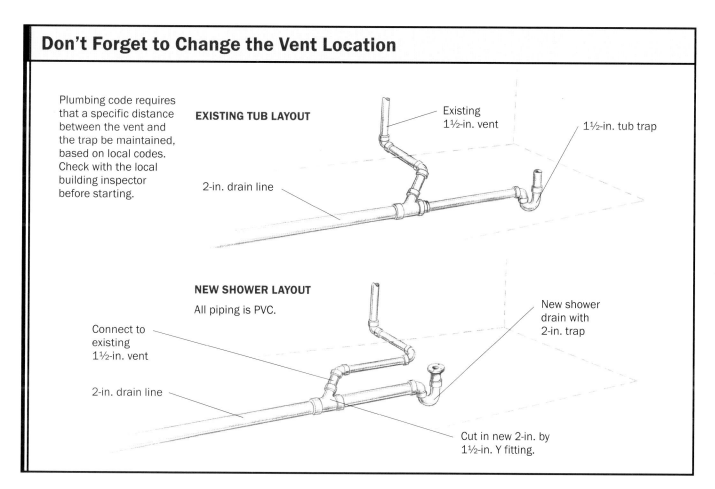

EXISTING TUB LAYOUT

Existing 1½-in. vent

1½-in. tub trap

2-in. drain line

NEW SHOWER LAYOUT

All piping is PVC.

Connect to existing 1½-in. vent

2-in. drain line

New shower drain with 2-in. trap

Cut in new 2-in. by 1½-in. Y fitting.

Tile Backerboard: HardiBacker, Durock, and DensShield

Backerboard panels provide a flat, firm base for the installation of tile. They are resistant to the effects of water exposure, including swelling, rot, and mold growth, and they can be used in fire-resistant assemblies. Each type of backerboard costs roughly the same and is available in similar dimensions at most lumberyards. However, each has characteristics that affect where it can be installed and how tile is placed on it.

HardiBacker

Composition: HardiBacker is made of cellulose fibers that are layered with cement slurry and cured through high-pressure autoclaving. The boards are also infused with additives to inhibit mold growth.

Weight: 2.6 lb. per sq. ft. (½ in. thick)

Mortar: Modified latex thinset should be used on HardiBacker. This type of thinset is more expensive than nonmodified products and also sets up faster—a benefit when working with large, heavy tile.

Installation: HardiBacker is best cut with carbon-tipped sawblades or specialty cutting shears and fastened to studs or joists with 1½-in. corrosion-resistant screws or nails.

Notes: HardiBacker has a smooth surface that allows the panel to be finished with products other than tile, including wallpaper and paint. This makes the panels useful for finished basements or garages that would benefit from the panels' moisture protection.

Durock

Composition: Durock panels have an aggregated portland-cement core and are wrapped with a polymer-coated, glass-fiber mesh.

Weight: 3 lb. per sq. ft. (½ in. thick)

Mortar: Tile can be set with modified latex thinset or nonmodified dry-set mortar. The latter is a less expensive option with a longer working time.

Installation: Durock is best cut with carbon-tipped sawblades or specialty cutting shears and fastened to studs or joists with 1½-in. corrosion-resistant screws or nails.

Notes: Unlike other backerboard, Durock meets industry standards for resistance to freeze/thaw cycles, allowing it to be used in exterior applications.

Same purpose, different applications. Not all backerboard is designed to be used in the same locations. Used incorrectly, the product can fail, causing the appearance and structural integrity of your walls or floors to suffer.

DensShield

Composition: Dens-Shield is a blend of glass fibers and gypsum sandwiched between two fiberglass mats. The front of the panel is faced with an acrylic coating that acts as a moisture barrier.

Weight: 2 lb. per sq. ft. (½ in. thick)

Mortar: As with HardiBacker, modified latex thinset should be used to set tile on DensShield panels.

Installation: DensShield can be cut with the same tools suggested for HardiBacker and Durock, or it can be scored and snapped like regular drywall. DensShield can be fastened to studs and joists with 1½-in. corrosion-resistant screws or nails.

Notes: Unlike other backerboard, DensShield can't be used where extreme levels of heat and moisture are common, such as in saunas or steam rooms.

Rob Yagid is an associate editor at Fine Homebuilding.

The hardest piece to remove surrounds the drain; here, practicing a little patience and cutting smaller pieces help. Once I've cut out around the drain, I reach down and undo the drain assembly with a wrench.

Relocating the Drain for the New Pan

Once the old tub is removed, the drain typically must be moved from the tub end to the center of the new shower pan (see the left photo on p. 152). After I open the subfloor, the plumber can reroute the drain and vent to the new position (see the drawing on p. 153).

Backerboard Creates a Water-Resistant Substrate

Unlike moisture-resistant gypsum-based products, cement backerboard can't come apart, even if it's soaking wet. Unless the installation is for a commercial steam shower, I don't use a vapor barrier between the framing and the backerboard. My experience tells me that any water vapor that does end up in the stud bays won't react with the backer or thinset and will evaporate quickly.

I make sure to use the largest pieces possible. Fewer pieces equals fewer joints, which minimizes any potential for water problems. I attach the backerboard with 1½-in. galvanized roofing nails or screw, and don't put any fasteners lower than 2 in. above the threshold to avoid leaks (see the photos on p. 153).

The Details: Make a Tile Shower Sparkle

The difference between an average tile job and an outstanding one is often a matter of a few relatively inexpensive details that don't require lots of time but can really personalize the bath area.

SOAP DISH

The author installed a little limestone soap dish into notches cut across the tops of two tiles. (If you're using ceramic tile, solid-surface material works, too.) He squared up the corners and sanded down the front edge, then cut three 2-in.-long slots for a drain.

SHAMPOO SHELF

When laying out the shampoo shelf, first determine where the full tiles will land to keep tile cuts to a minimum. A vacuum helps remove dust as the backerboard is cut.

DECORATIVE BORDER

Used for an accent, small mesh-backed tiles are easier to install if they're first mounted on a piece of waterproof membrane with binding-fortified thinset. The membrane also brings the small tiles flush with the big ones.

CORNER SEAT

Available in different sizes (see "Sources" on p. 158), the galvanized-steel seat form is screwed into the framing behind the backerboard at a height of 18 in. from the floor.

2

Remove the waste, then reinforce the opening with 2× scrap material secured to the backerboard with construction adhesive and galvanized screws.

3

After coating the recess with thinset, cover the inside with a piece of waterproof membrane, folding and sealing corners as needed. Prefab inserts are also available.

4

Starting with the bottom piece, line the recess with tile, followed in order by the back, top, and sides. All pieces should be back-coated with a layer of thinset.

2

The next day, when the thinset has dried, the assembly is cut into uniform strips two tiles wide and to a length that matches the width of the large tiles.

3

The strips now can be applied to the backerboard with a liberal coating of thinset.

2

The form then is filled with mud, which creates the substrate for the tile. After the top is leveled off, the mud is left to dry overnight.

3

After the mud is prepped with successive layers of thinset, waterproof membrane, and thinset, tile is laid across the top, then the front. Temporary braces keep the edge tile in place until the thinset bonds.

Sources

American Standard
800-442-1902
www.americanstandard-us.
com
Acrylic/fiberglass
shower pans

Aqua Glass®
800-632-0911
www.aquaglass.com

Aquatic
800–877-2005
www.aquaticbath.com

Georgia-Pacific
800-225-6119
www.gp.com
DensShield

Innovis Corporation
916-361-2601
www.innoviscorp.com
Better-Bench®, galva-
nized-steel seat form

James Hardie
888-JHARDIE
www.jameshardie.com
HardiBacker

**Laticrete
International Inc.**
800-243-4788
www.laticrete.com
Thinsets

Noble Company
800-878-5788
www.noblecompany.com
Chlorinated polyethyl-
ene waterproof
membrane

ProSpec® American
800-334-0784
www.prospec.com

USG
800-874-4968
www.usg.com
Durock

Prefab Shower Pans

Tile ready: a prefab pan of rein-
forced backerboard.

Fiberglass: inexpensive but the
least durable.

Acrylic: a tougher skin than
fiberglass.

Shower Pans: Build Your Own or Buy Them Ready Made

I like to build my shower pans with a waterproof membrane and built-up mud floor (see
the photo above right). I think this type of
pan makes the best substrate for a tile floor
because it's solid, won't crack, and can conform to fit any space.

But if you want something faster, you can
buy a prefab pan that you still can tile over.
Made of waterproof extruded polystyrene
and backerboard, these pans have floors that
slope uniformly to a built-in drain and are
relatively easy to install.

A shower doesn't always have to have a
tiled floor and threshold; often, a homeowner
just wants a simpler look. Options include
prefab shower pans made of fiberglass and
acrylic that look fine with most tile jobs (see
the sidebar above). They come in standard
sizes that fit many, but not all, installations
and are found in most plumbing-supply
houses and home centers.

Tom Meehan *is a second-generation tile installer*
who has been installing tile for more than 35 years.
Tom lives with his wife, Lane, and their four sons
in Harwich, Massachusetts, where they own Cape
Cod Tileworks.

Putting the Craft Back in a Craftsman Bath

■ BY JERRI HOLAN

As an architect who works on older homes, I spend a lot of time fixing past "improvements" to kitchens and baths. My clients' Craftsman-style house is a perfect example. During the 1970s, its second-floor guest bath received a makeover that included dark brown floor tiles, laminate counters, and a shadow-casting partition over the tub (see the inset photo on p. 161). Our goal was to return this bathroom to its Craftsman roots and cheer it up with light finishes, modern fixtures, and new tilework in sympathy with the home's original look (see the photo at right on p. 160).

The house was built in 1905, just as the formality of Victorian architecture was relaxing into the Craftsman style. During this period, both styles shared some types of signature finish materials, especially ceramic tile. The 1-in. hexagonal floor tiles and the 3-in. by 6-in. subway wall tiles the homeowners chose for this project fall into this category.

From the outset, we knew that tile was going to set the tone for this bathroom. So we pored over traditional tile patterns for decorative touches and looked at a multitude of color selections. In the end, we settled on white for the field tile as the best way to brighten the room. And to give the floor character and to emphasize its shape, we devised a border detail of dark green tiles linked at the corners by a detail composed of hexagonal tiles in an abstract flower pattern (see the photos on pp. 160 and 161).

The Frame Remains the Same as Tiling Tricks Lower Costs

Restorations can get pricey quickly, especially when structural and plumbing changes crop up. With that in mind, we decided early on not to relocate plumbing fixtures.

You can expect a few sags here and there in an old house. We had our share, with an

Bold lines hide the deviations. The tapered white tiles along the edges of the floor and at the base of the walls barely register (right). Instead, you look at the strong geometry of the borders and corner patterns. At the doorway, a tapered threshold reveals the sloping floor (above).

"From the outset, we knew that tile was going to set the tone for this bathroom."

out-of-square floor that sloped enough to drain and walls that were distinctly out of plumb. The structure was still sound, however, which was good news for the budget and an opportunity for our tilesetters (Riley Doty and his associate, Jane Aeon) to use some tricks of the tile trade to hide the framing anomalies.

Before installing the tile, they brought the floor closer to level by adding a base layer of tile backerboard to the subfloor, followed by a tapered layer of mortar. You can see the extent of the built-up base in the threshold at the entry to the bath (see the left photo above).

The out-of-square corners were handled differently. Rows of 1-in.-sq. white tiles between the borders and the walls are tapered as necessary to meet the wall. But because the eye is drawn to the dark stripes

Light by the window, but nowhere else. An ungainly partition and a plywood sink cabinet were among the unpleasant details in this 1970s remodel.

BEFORE

AFTER

Borders and bright finishes. Striped borders of green and white tiles lead the eye in and around the new bath. Lowering the partition next to the tub lets in more daylight. The shower curtain now rides on an L-shaped curtain rod.

Sources

Daltile
214-398-1411
www.daltile.com
Mosaic floor tiles

Kohler
Memoirs® collection
800-456-4537
www.kohler.com
Toilet and lavatory

Chicago Faucets®
model #746-374
847-803-5000
www.chicagofaucets.
com
Lavatory faucet

Rejuvenation®
St. Helens collection
888-401-1900
www.rejuvenation.com
Wall sconces

Tips for Working with Mosaic Tiles

MOSAICIST'S TAPE

ENLARGED SAW CART

SUPPORT TILE EDGES

Mosaic tiles present installers with a distinct set of challenges. They are fragile to cut, and once they've been separated from their backing, they can be difficult to handle. On this job, we did three things to make the job go more smoothly.

First, we used mosaicist's tape to collate the border tiles into tidy groupings (above left). This sticky film allowed us to mount strips or loose groups of individual tiles bottom-side up into custom configurations on the job site.

Second, we enlarged the saw's cart with a piece of Corian® countertop.

(above center). This big sled allowed us to rest an entire sheet of tiles on the cutting surface.

Third, we supported tiles from below as we cut them. With a standard tile saw, the blade travels in a $\frac{3}{8}$-in.-wide gap. That's okay for large tiles, but for mosaics, it means the edges of the tiles aren't supported adequately. With our custom sled, the blade travels in a narrow, blade-wide kerf. We used a fine-grit glass-cutting blade, which carved gently through the mosaic tiles (above right).

—Riley Doty and Jane Aeon are tilesetters in Oakland, California.

in the borders, the skewed wall lines are minimized.

In a similar manner, the horizontal bands of green trim tiles on the wall establish strong, level sightlines. The tiles below them are tapered to adjust for the remaining slope in the floor. The finishing touches were to install compatible fixtures (see "Sources," above).

Our local preservation association liked the project well enough to give it an award in the historic-finishes category. Better yet, the clients are happy with it. This is good, because cost overruns with this phase meant that we'll have to wait a little longer to take on that 1970s kitchen downstairs.

Jerri Holan (www.holanarchitects.com) is an architect in the San Francisco Bay area.

Glass Tile

■ BY TOM MEEHAN

It has been used for centuries, but until recently, glass tile was relegated to museums and specialty shops. Today, it comes in an array of styles, from iridescent mosaics to luminous squares of recycled and sandblasted beer bottles (see "A Peek Into the World of Glass Tile" on p. 168). Tile shops like mine see glass-tile sales double every year. However, lots of folks are in for a shock if they try to install it like

ceramic tile: The thinset and its application are different; the paper backing for small tiles is stuck to the front, not to the back of the tiles; and timing becomes an important part of the job.

Layout Needs Room to Move

On this particular job, the shower area was to be covered with 1-in. tiles grouped into 12-in.-sq. sheets. When I work with small tiles, I try to make sure that the backerboard is smooth and flat; any imperfections will show as bumps in the tile. This phenomenon is especially true with glass tiles, which catch the light even more than ceramic or stone. Once I've installed the backerboard, I seal the joints between the sheets with thinset and mesh tape, and then smooth any bumps with a steel floating trowel and thinset. The thinset should set overnight before the tile is installed.

When laying out a back wall, don't be tempted to squeeze the sheets together so that you can get a full tile and avoid cutting. Believe it or not, glass tiles expand and contract with changes in temperature, much more so than ceramic tiles. Direct sunlight can heat tiles enough to make them move. If tiles are too tight, any movement can make them pop off the wall or crack—or even crack the backerboard. I try to leave ¼ in. of space in each corner; intersecting walls hide the gap.

I begin the layout with a level horizontal line halfway up the back wall, equivalent to an even course of tile, which in this case worked out to be 48 in. from the top of the tub. This horizontal line serves not only as a reference for spacing but also, as you'll see later, marks the extent of the first round of applying the glass tile. Next, I measure up to determine the width of the row at the ceiling. Anything over a half piece works well, and I can adjust the cut to make up the difference when the ceiling is uneven.

Thinset? Make Mine Extra-Sticky

Because it's vitreous, glass doesn't absorb liquid like ceramic tile, and it requires a higher grade of acrylic or latex-modified thinset to bond to the backerboard. Most glass-tile manufacturers specify what brands of thinset to use. Because the tile often is translucent, the thinset should be white; gray mixes darken the tile's color. Any pattern the trowel leaves in the thinset will show through, too, so the thinset must be spread and leveled with a ³⁄₁₆-in. V-notch trowel, and then smoothed out (see "Troweling" on the facing page).

I start laying the tile sheets from the level line, and then work down rather than working with a full sheet off the tub. If the tub is out of level, it's easier to adjust the cuts as measured from the course above. Once I press the sheets into the thinset and finish the half wall, I use a block of wood and a hammer to bed the tile fully and evenly into the thinset. You also can use a beater block (a wooden block padded on one side with a piece of rubber, available from most tile distributors) and a rubber mallet. I make any cuts with a wet saw (see the bottom photo on p. 166) fitted with a diamond blade; a pair of tile nippers is handy to make minor adjustments in a cut.

Timing Is Crucial When Removing Paper Facing

The main reason I don't install too much glass tile at one time is that while the thinset is wet, I need to move individual tiles and erase any pattern inadvertently created by the 12-in. tile sheets. But first I have to peel off the paper facing carefully so that I don't disturb the majority of tiles.

After waiting 15 minutes to 20 minutes for the thinset to bond, I wet the paper with

Troveling

Many glass tiles are translucent, so you need to use white thinset because gray will show through and darken the tile. With a 3/16-in. V-notch trowel, roughly distribute the thinset over a small area (photo 1). Even out the material using the trowel's notched edge (photo 2), then smooth the ridges (photo 3) so that they won't show through the tile.

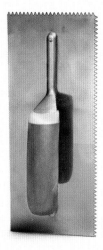

Even out the thinset.

1 Spread thinset on the wall.

3 Smooth the ridges.

Setting

Many varieties of small glass field tile are held together in sheets by a paper facing on the front (photo 1) rather than a mesh fabric on the back. (Mesh on the back might be visible through the translucent material.) To make a wall of tile appear unified and not look like a grid of 12-in. squares, the paper must be removed and individual tiles adjusted to mask the pattern.

The trick lies in waiting for the thinset to become tacky; in normal conditions, this might be 15 minutes or 20 minutes. If the thinset is allowed to dry beyond that time, say an hour, the bond becomes more fragile, and more tiles will pull off with the paper. If the thinset is left to dry overnight, the bond sets, and the tile will be impossible to adjust.

First wet the paper with a sponge dampened with warm water (photo 2); after a few minutes, the water-based glue softens, and the paper can be peeled off gently (photo 3).

During the process of peeling the paper, individual tiles will fall off occasionally (photo 4). A quick coat of thinset on the tile's back is enough to set it back in place.

Simple jig for cutting small tile

Cut with a wet saw, small glass tiles often are difficult to hold and cut accurately. The author makes an L-shaped cut in a larger piece of tile and uses it as a jig that holds the smaller tiles in line with the sawblade.

Set the tile.

Dampen the paper.

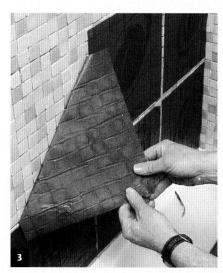

Peel carefully.

Make an easy fix.

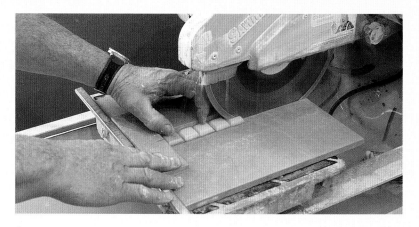

Grouting

Each tile manufacturer specifies what type of grout to use on a particular tile. After the grout is spread (photo 1) and has set up for about 20 minutes, wipe away the excess with cheesecloth or paper towels (photo 2). A sponge dampened with clean water (photo 3) works well to clean any residue from the tile.

2 Wipe the excess.

3 Clean the tile.

1 Pack the seams.

a sponge and warm water. After a minute or so, the paper can be pulled off slowly, downward at an angle. One or two tiles may pop off, but that's no big deal; I just stick them back in place with a dab of thinset.

The trickiest part of this process is that the timing varies according to the room's temperature and humidity. Heat and dry conditions make the thinset bond faster and give me less time to work, so I start to check the bond in an inconspicuous place after about 10 minutes. If the tiles move around too easily as I peel off a bit of paper, I know that I should wait a few more minutes.

Once the paper is off, the glass tiles must be examined to make sure none have slipped.

Never wait until the next day to remove the paper; the tiles have to be examined and straightened while the thinset is fresh (see "Setting" on the facing page).

When Grouting, Less Water Is Better

After the thinset has bonded fully for 48 hours, the tile must be washed to prepare it for grouting. I use a nylon-bristle brush and a sponge with warm water to clean any residue or paper backing from the surface of the tile. I use a utility knife to remove any excess thinset in the joints, but I'm careful when doing so; glass tile scratches easily.

A Peek into the World of Glass Tile

Glass tile is versatile stuff; it's available in styles that range from clear to opaque, from glossy and iridescent to the eroded look of beach glass.

Colors range from gaudy lollipop primaries to muted earth tones and just about every shade in between. Commonly seen in sheets of 1-in. squares, glass tile now is made in sizes that approximate ceramic tiles (2-in., 4-in., and even 12-in. squares), as well as rectangles, textured borders, and tiny mosaics. And like ceramics, it can be used on walls, counters, and floors, although glass tiles used on floors should have a matte finish or texture that makes them slip-proof.

One big factor to consider: Glass is more likely to show scratches than ceramics or stone; finishes applied to the tile are susceptible to scratches, too.

Texture with a Variety of Color

These 4-in.-sq., clear-glass tiles from Architectural Glass, Inc.™ (see "Sources" on p. 170) have textured faces and ribbed backs; a glaze bonded to the tile backs gives them their color. The company also offers a higher-end integral color tile and custom designs.

Broad Palette of Recycled Color

Fireclay Tile (see "Sources") makes mosaic, field, and specialty tile from 100 percent recycled glass in 36 different shades of integral color, glossy or matte. They also offer custom border and mosaic designs.

Grouting glass tiles is not difficult, but again, it's different from grouting ceramic tile. Some manufacturers specify sanded or non-sanded grout; here, I used a recommended sanded grout in a color that complemented the tile. After I spread the grout on the walls, I let it set for about 20 minutes; the wait is longer than for ceramic tile because the glass tile doesn't absorb moisture from the grout.

Before starting to clean with water, I use cheesecloth or paper towels to rub down the walls to get rid of any extra grout and to fill in any voids between the tiles. This dry method also lets me clean the surface without adding any extra moisture that might dilute the grout.

Once the tile is wiped down, I go back over it with clean water and a damp sponge

Iridescence

Oceanside Glasstile® (see "Sources") offers a variety of tile ranging from 1-in.-sq. mosaics to 5-in. by 5-in. field tiles, specialty borders, and decorative single tiles. Many feature a metallic glaze that's applied to the surface of the tile.

Solid Colors in Mosaics

Hakatai® (see "Sources") sells mesh-backed mosaics (instead of paper-faced) in ¾-in. and 1-in. sizes in many opaque and solid colors. They also offer 2-in. squares of clear glass with color fired onto the tile back and irregularly shaped pebbles.

Earth Tones in Recycled Glass

Made from 100% recycled content, Bedrock® tiles (see "Sources" on p. 170) are available in many sizes, from 2-in. squares to 5-in. by 10-in. rectangles to hexagonal shapes. Finish can be glossy or matte, but the color is integral and ranges from clear to solidly opaque.

to do a finer cleaning and to reduce any topical film. Less water is better. As in any grouting job, it's important to strike corners or intersections of wall and tile with a trowel or putty knife to make sure these joints are tight and neat. Once everything is set and a slight film has developed over the tile, I use a rag to bring the glass tile to a shine. I try not to wait more than 15 minutes after sponging; any longer, and the film starts to set up and becomes too hard to remove easily (see "Grouting," on p. 167).

Simple Tip for Smoothing Tile

Instead of using a specialized edge tile, the author sometimes runs the field tile to the wall edge and smooths any sharp edges with a diamond-impregnated pad.

Sources

Architectural Glass Inc.
845-733-4720
www.architecturalglassinc.com

Bedrock Industries
877-283-7625
www.bedrockindustries.com

Hakatai Enterprises Inc.
888-667-2429
www.hakatai.com

Miracle Sealants Company
800-350-1901
www.miraclesealants.com
511 Impregnator

Oceanside Glasstile
760-929-4000
www.glasstile.com

Fireclay Tile
www.fireclaytile.com

Cleaning and Sealing Are Just as Important as Thinset and Grout

A day or two after grouting, I smooth exposed tile edges with a diamond-abrasive pad, and then clean the tile with a commercial tile cleaner. I wet down the walls before applying the cleaner and also protect any chrome or brass plumbing fixtures with tape and plastic bags. Rather than use stronger cleaners that might compromise the grout, I use a fine, nylon scrubbing pad to clean off heavy grout residue. I always give the walls a double rinse to flush away any cleaner residue.

Sealing grout is simple and should not be overlooked; it helps keep grout lines from absorbing mildew and other stains. I use a wet, clean cloth rag and apply a double coat of sealer on the grout and tile as well. I then towel off the wall with a dry rag. I used Miracle Sealants 511 Impregnator (see "Sources" at left) on this project. One key to sealing walls is to start from the bottom and work up from floor to ceiling to avoid streaking. Once the sealer is dry, glass-tile maintenance is minimal; I use dish soap and water to clean it on a regular basis.

Tom Meehan is a second-generation tile installer who has been installing tile for more than 35 years. Tom lives with his wife, Lane, and their four sons in Harwich, Massachusetts, where they own Cape Cod Tileworks.

Master Bath with a Twist

BY CHET ZEBROSKI

My wife, Holly, and I live in a typical 1960s-style ranch in a town north of San Francisco. The house has 8-ft. ceilings, dark, narrow hallways, and small bathrooms. The homes in our neighborhood delivered a lot of house for the dollar, but stylish they are not.

Now that our kids have moved on to lives of their own, we're looking at our house with different eyes—eyes that see potential in every outdated space. Deciding where to begin remodeling was easy: The master bath had to come first.

An iridescent backdrop. Glass-mosaic tiles that change color with viewing angle and time of day blanket the back wall of the shower. Creamy, sandstone-colored walls provide a neutral surround for the dazzling tile. Photo taken at A on floor plan (see p. 182).

Step into the Stretch Remo

Even by 1960s standards, the master bath was a squeeze for two people. Once you passed through the 24-in.-wide doorway, a frosted-glass shower enclosure and an institutional fluorescent-light ceiling grid conspired to make the room feel smaller than its 18 sq. ft. of floor space (see the "Before" floor plan below). Expanding the master bath with an addition was out of the question. We didn't want to lose any of our precious backyard space, the only logical place to expand. And we couldn't justify the extra expense, given the other improvements that we plan to make.

The challenge boiled down to finding a way to expand the feeling of the bathroom without expanding its size much, and devising a floor plan that delivered a little more elbow room at rush hour. We met the challenge by grabbing a bit of the hall closet on the inboard side, letting in sunshine with a skylight over the shower (see the photo on p. 171), and stretching the bathroom's footprint to the edge of the roof overhang (see the "After" floor plan below).

Just enough bench. A triangular cast-concrete shelf in the shower makes a convenient spot to sit and soak. Both bathroom and shower floors are slate, offset at the corners to include glass-tile insets. Photo taken at B on floor plan.

Bath Expands at Both Ends

A triangular space carved out of the hall closet made room for a bench in the shower. On the opposite side of the bathroom, where the lavatory reaches to the edge of the existing roofline, a mirror image of the triangle is reflected in the new windowsill. The lavatory counter follows this angle, creating a much larger doorway and a more generous sense of space.

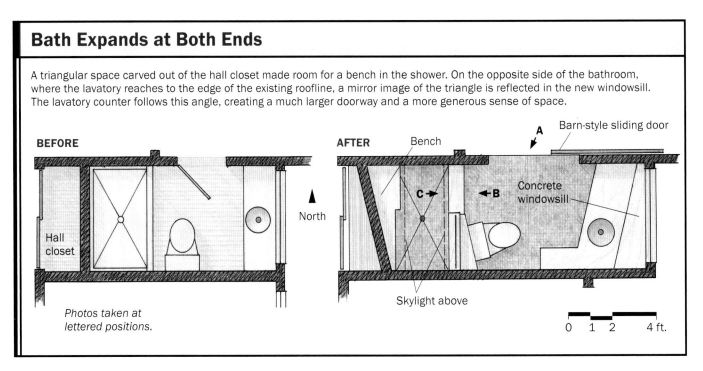

BEFORE

Hall closet

Photos taken at lettered positions.

North

AFTER

Bench

A

Barn-style sliding door

C→

←B

Concrete windowsill

Skylight above

0 1 2 4 ft.

Daylight and Multiple Ceiling Heights

Varying ceiling heights over the shower, the primary space, and the lavatory give this small bath a larger presence.

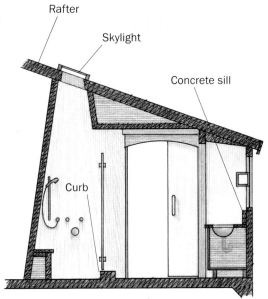

Rafter

Skylight

Concrete sill

Curb

The east-side extension.
The lavatory bump-out, with its triangular windowsill and concrete counter, reaches into the space below the existing eaves. A 4-ft.-wide opening to the hall on the left is closed with a door that rolls on a barn-door track. On the right, abstract flowers of glass tile and brass rods spring from the base of the shower partition. Photo taken at C on floor plan.

Include a Convenient Place to Sit in the Shower

As we pondered the plan, Holly and I considered the idea of a bench in the shower (see the photo on the facing page). It's a great place to sit and let the water pour over you, or to perch a leg for a soapy scrub. When we realized that we could annex a triangular piece of an adjacent hall closet,

we turned it into a bench in the corner of our new shower. The wall above it torques into a rectangular skylight well as it climbs to the roof, creating a twisting backdrop of glass tile.

The shape of the bench is repeated at the opposite end of the room, where a triangular concrete windowsill sits atop the lavatory counter's backsplash. The cabinet below reflects this shape, creating a floor that is wider on the hallway side and making it easier to get into and out of the room.

Concrete ripples in the counter. Resembling the impressions left by retreating waves on a sandy beach, slight level changes in the concrete step back from a hammered-copper sink bowl.

A Neutral Palette Lets the Tile Take Center Stage

A little iridescent tile goes a long way and needs subdued surroundings. We flanked the tile with white-plaster walls and ceilings tinted with a bit of ochre to give the plaster some warmth. Our plaster contractor, Alfonso Bazurto, persuaded us to fortify the plaster with an acrylic additive called Quikrete® to resist mold, mildew, and cracking. So far, it has worked.

We chose 2-ft.-sq. slates as floor tiles to minimize the number of grid lines. (More lines make a floor seem smaller.) Like the shower tiles, the slates are steel blue and rusty red. They are offset at their corners just enough to inset a glass tile.

Holly and I have a strong admiration for concrete, with its sturdy presence and ability to take on any shape imaginable. We hired David Condon of Kilnworks to cast the shower bench, the curb, the windowsill, and the lavatory counter (see the photo above). The concrete counter's delicately eroded edges, created with thin layers of hardboard glued to the inside of the countertop mold, give the counter an almost geological bearing.

Chet Zebroski is a partner in Erickson Zebroski Design Group in San Francisco (www.ezdg.net).

Sources

Glass mosaics:
www.glasstile.com

Lavatory sink:
www.oregoncopperbowl.com

Acrylic fortifier:
www.quikrete.com

Capture Adjacent Space with a Big Door and a Garden View

All designers have their tricks. An old standby is to make a small room seem larger by making it a part of another room. We played that card by taking advantage of the new, wide opening to the bathroom. Instead of a swinging door, we installed a 4-ft. 6-in.-wide barn-style door on a track. When the door is fully open, the hallway seems a part of the bath.

We have a private backyard to the east, so we included the largest possible window over the sink. Then we lowered the ceiling a bit to give this part of the room its own sense of place (see the photo on p. 173). The window faces the sunrise and a small sculpture garden that greets us every morning.

A Skylight Cheers Up an Attic Bath

■ BY SCOTT DONAHUE

Of all the rooms in this old house, built in 1916, the third-floor bath had the worst layout. The room measured less than 5 ft. wide by 11 ft. long, and the tub was tucked between floor-to-ceiling sidewalls. Getting to the toilet required squeezing through a 14-in.-wide passageway between the tub and the sink.

I wanted to improve circulation and bring some light into this dark, cramped shooting gallery of a bath. The partition walls flanking the bathtub had to go, and I considered replacing the built-in tub with a freestanding claw-foot model. But no one was wild about having a shower curtain as the centerpiece of the bathroom. The only alternative was tucking the tub into the adjacent attic.

I took some measurements and discovered there was just enough headroom under the roof for a tub where a person of average height could shower comfortably (see the drawing on p. 177). Compared to the cast-iron alternative, the lightweight acrylic tub chosen for the bath alcove (BainUltra®, jetless Meridian™ 55; www.bainultra.com) was considerably easier to carry up three flights of narrow stairs.

Capping the alcove with a skylight went a long way toward brightening the room. Almost as an afterthought, I decided to make the skylight operable, which added more headroom (Velux® GPL roof window; www.veluxusa.com). When it's fully open, whoever is in the shower has an unimpeded view of the sunrise over the Oakland Hills.

Scott Donahue is an architect based in Oakland, California.

A narrow space gains breathing room. A tapered sink counter and a low privacy wall screening the toilet help to counteract the room's long, narrow plan. The original medicine cabinet and Douglas-fir floors are ready for another 100 years of service.

Small expansion, big payoff. Centered between the existing rafters, a 30-in. by 55-in. operable skylight provides ventilation, daylight, and adjustable headroom in this tub/shower alcove tucked into unused attic space. Shelves for towels and a narrow bench made of cedar 2×4s on edge occupy the space between the rim of the tub and the original wall plane. The 2×4s are supported by L-brackets screwed to the wall framing.

Bathed in Light

Floor-to-ceiling walls flanking the built-in tub made this narrow bathroom seem even smaller, and getting to the loo meant squeezing past the sink. Tucked into the adjacent attic, the new bathtub frees up space for a sink with a wedge-shaped counter that contributes to the room's open feeling. An operable skylight above the tub maximizes headroom and natural light. Access to attic storage is maintained via a new hatch on a bedroom wall.

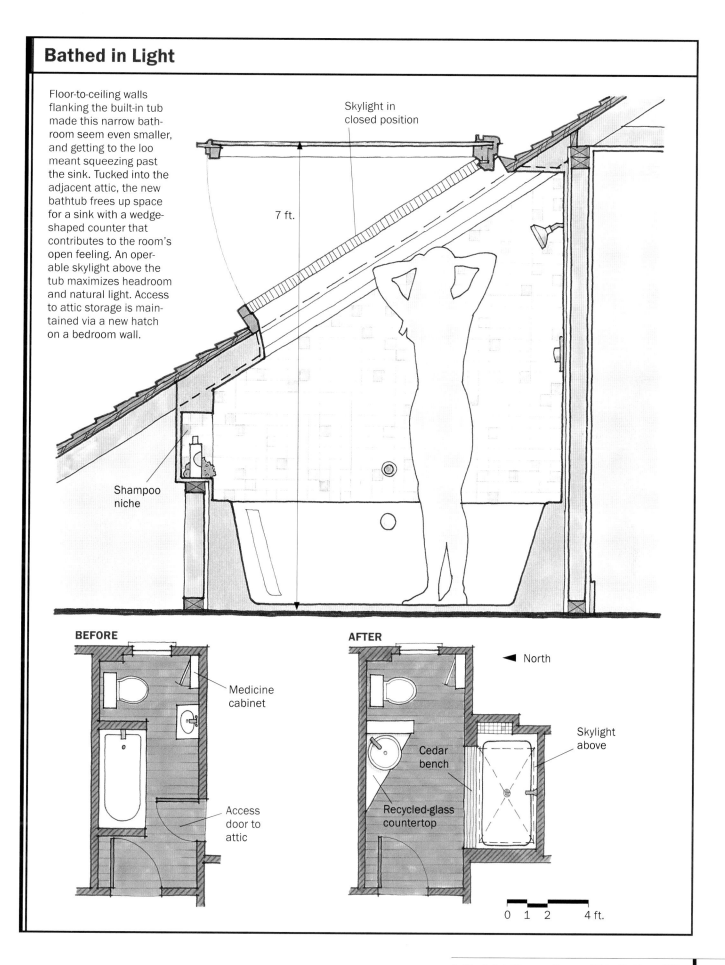

Skylight in closed position

7 ft.

Shampoo niche

BEFORE

Medicine cabinet

Access door to attic

AFTER

◀ North

Cedar bench

Recycled-glass countertop

Skylight above

0 1 2 4 ft.

Brighten Up a Small Bath

■ BY MAAIKE LINNENKAMP

The only bathroom in this small ranch-style house was cluttered, dark, and uninspiring. Besides changing the aesthetics, the main challenges were bringing in more daylight, increasing storage, and giving the bath a much-needed sense of spaciousness. The bold stroke is a 2-ft.-deep bay that extends beyond the original exterior wall. The bay created space for a shower bench, room for a towel rack out of the spray pattern, and a place for a generous frosted-acrylic window that offers privacy, light, and ventilation. Storage is provided by a custom cabinet recessed into the bay. A totemic floor-to-ceiling glass-tile inlay surrounded by alabaster floor and wall tile injects a prominent centerpiece.

These elements are the most obvious changes that transformed this bath. But they are only part of the story. A supporting cast of less obvious details and principles is making quieter contributions. Here are the lessons, both large and small, of this little bath.

Maaike Linnenkamp is president of NBI Design Inc. (www.nbidesign.com) in Los Gatos, California.

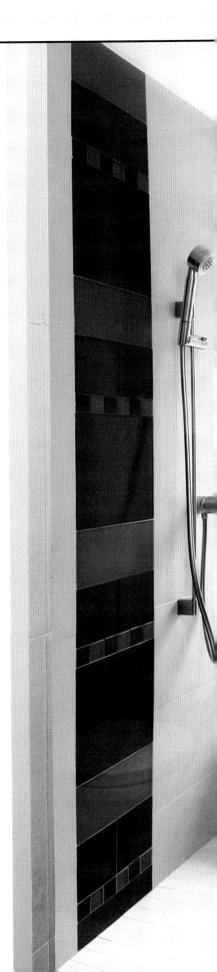

Maximize daylight while maintaining privacy. Acrylic-block windows are lightweight and unbreakable; this awning-style version lets in fresh air. Tubular skylights are another great way to bring daylight inside. They are less expensive than conventional skylights, are less prone to leakage, and can eliminate the need for electric light during the day. Both options maintain a high level of privacy.

Create Multipurpose Features

Besides accommodating a seating area and storage space, the bay provides ventilation, natural light, and extended sightlines during the day. The storage built-in is a focal point upon entry, especially at night.

Push outside the box

In the bay bump-out, an **awning-style window** glazed with acrylic mimics the look of glass blocks, without the weight. The window's wavy pattern preserves privacy.

Support brackets bear on the original foundation, a feature that simplified construction and made it easier to get a permit. The foundation didn't have to be extended into the side-yard setback.

Replace the Crammed Tub/Shower Combination

Bathing has become less popular, so the argument that you need a tub for resale value doesn't wash anymore. Compared to a bathtub that visually divides the room, glass shower doors make the space seem larger and more inclusive. A code-compliant shower also uses less water than a tub.

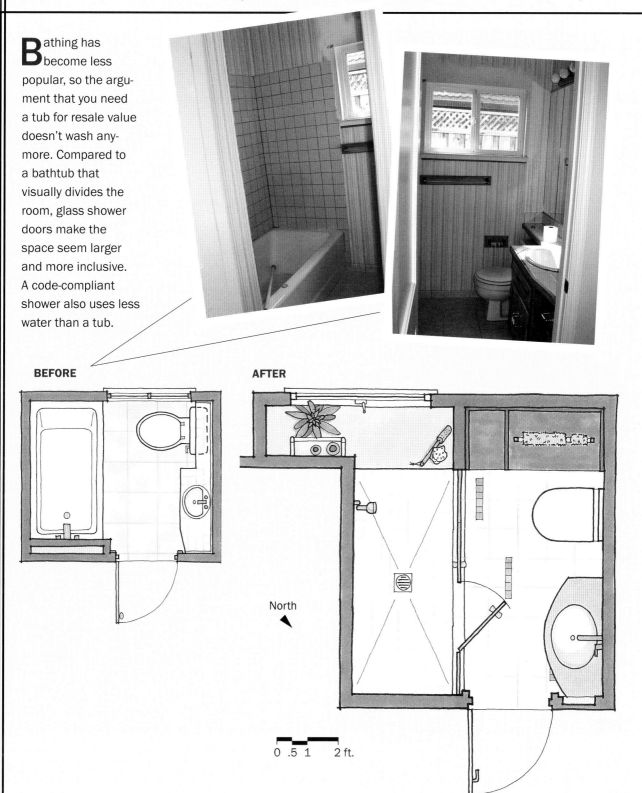

BEFORE

AFTER

North ◀

0 .5 1   2 ft.

Install a Dual-Flush Toilet

The amount of water that goes through in a regular flush is significant. A dual-flush option is available on many models now, so efficiency doesn't have to entail a design compromise.

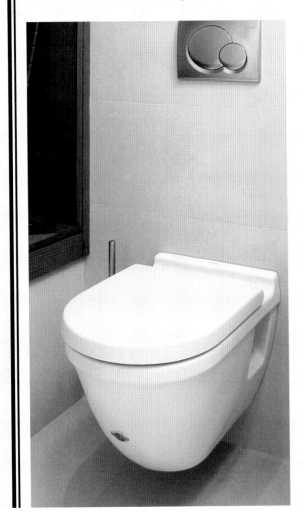

Use Large Tiles

In small baths, large tiles with very thin grout lines make the room look bigger. Plus, the tile is easier to clean.

Sources

Fixtures
Hansgrohe
Axor® Series faucet, model 38117821;
shower valve, model 35375801; shower bar,
model 27941800
www.hansgrohe-usa.com

Toilet
Duravit bowl, Starck 3, www.duravit.com;
Geberit® tank, www.chicagofaucets.com

Tubular skylight
Solatube®, www.solatube.com

Tubular skylight window
Hy-Lite® acrylic-block awning style, www.hy-lite.com

Hang the Cabinetry and the Toilet

Elevating the cabinets and the commode makes everything easier to clean and saves space. The room looks larger if the floor tile is undisturbed throughout the footprint of the bathroom.

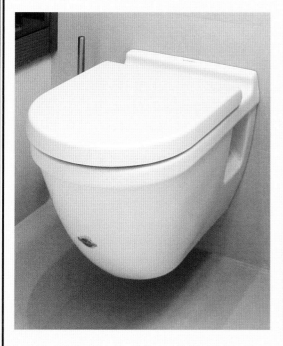

Get Creative with Cabinetry

Stereotypical kitchen cabinetry doesn't have a place in the bathroom. Instead, the cabinetry can be a distinctive feature, both functional and good-looking.

Pair a Harmonious, Natural Color Palette with Sophisticated Accents

This design approach will make the bathroom personal, timeless, and comfortable and will reduce the chances that you'll become annoyed at some point by either blandness or an overpowering color choice.

Install a Bathroom Fan

■ BY MIKE GUERTIN

If you're like me and enjoy a hot shower, the last thing you want in your bathroom is a fan that sounds like a helicopter. But hot showers create moisture that, left alone, will lead to mold and mildew. Lucky for us, the bathroom fan has come of age.

Today's fans are quieter and move more air than yesterday's models. Whether I'm building a new house or remodeling a bathroom, I install an ultra-quiet exhaust fan because a quiet fan is more likely to be used. Also, a properly installed fan clears excess moisture from the bathroom and the house to where it is unable to find a way back in. The fan should be near the shower, and the ductwork should be vented out the roof or a gable-end wall. Vapor exhausted through a soffit often will be drawn back into the attic through the soffit vents. The entire system must be airtight to keep moisture from leaking into the attic or wall and ceiling cavities.

Once installed, the fan must be used properly. As long as moisture is in the bathroom, the fan should continue to run. To eliminate the risk of the fan being left on for hours at a time, I install a delay-timer switch that turns off the fan up to an hour after it first was turned on.

This may sound like a lot of work for a bathroom that has a window in it. But as a remodeler, I've seen the mold and mildew problems that moisture can cause. Opening a window is a good idea, but it isn't reliable enough to eradicate moisture effectively.

Mike Guertin, a contributing editor to Fine Homebuilding, lives in Rhode Island.

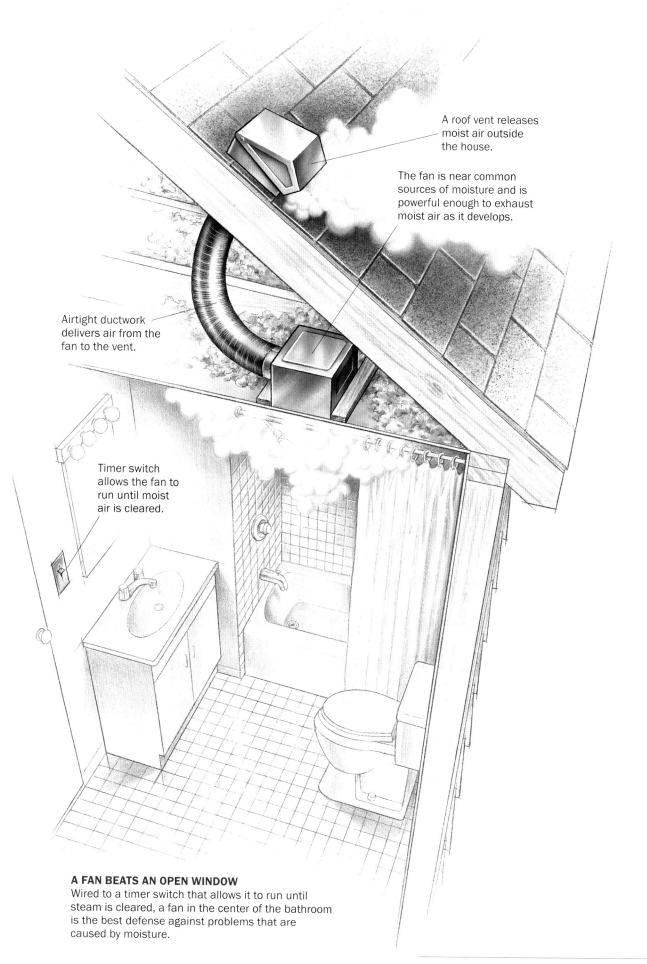

A roof vent releases moist air outside the house.

The fan is near common sources of moisture and is powerful enough to exhaust moist air as it develops.

Airtight ductwork delivers air from the fan to the vent.

Timer switch allows the fan to run until moist air is cleared.

A FAN BEATS AN OPEN WINDOW
Wired to a timer switch that allows it to run until steam is cleared, a fan in the center of the bathroom is the best defense against problems that are caused by moisture.

Protect the Bathroom and Yourself

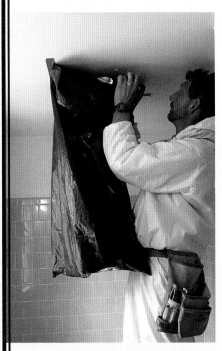

Cheap and easy dust containment. A garbage bag taped to the bathroom ceiling catches dust while the ceiling is cut. A plastic suit (available at paint stores for less than $10) protects your skin from fiberglass insulation and dust in the attic.

Use a template and blocking for accuracy and convenience. Mark the cut in the attic with a cardboard template cut from the fan's box. Then screw a piece of blocking to the drywall to catch the scrap when it is cut free. Leave the screw loose so that you can twist the blocking out of the saw's path.

Today's Fans Are Stronger, Yet Quieter Than Ever

Walk into any big-box store, and you'll find dozens of bathroom fans priced from $20 to $200. Here are a few important things to consider when choosing a fan.

Power
For an average-size bathroom, the Home Ventilation Institute recommends that the fan exhaust 1 cfm (cubic foot per minute) per square foot of bathroom.

Sound Level
Sones are the measure of sound for bathroom fans. Normal conversation takes place from 3 sones to 4 sones. Some bath fans are quieter than 1 sone.

Useful Features
Independently operating lights, heaters, and moisture sensors that turn on the fan as needed are nifty extras.

Venting: Get Vapor Out, and Keep It Out

The fan can exhaust air through the roof using a roof vent or out a gable-end wall using a clothes-dryer vent. Under no circumstances should the fan vent through or into the eaves or soffit. Airflow will draw vapor back into the attic through the soffit vents, making the fan little more than a waste of energy.

THROUGH THE ROOF

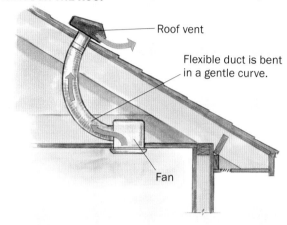

Roof vent

Flexible duct is bent in a gentle curve.

Fan

OUT THE WALL

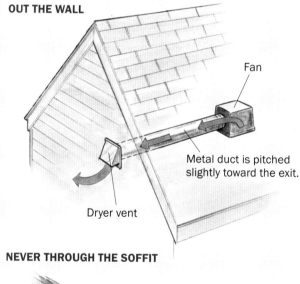

Fan

Metal duct is pitched slightly toward the exit.

Dryer vent

NEVER THROUGH THE SOFFIT

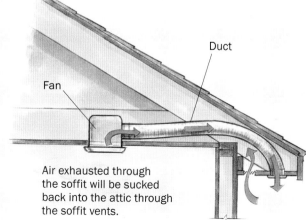

Duct

Fan

Air exhausted through the soffit will be sucked back into the attic through the soffit vents.

One Switch Controls the Light and Fan

Bathroom-fan-and-light combination units often are used to replace existing lights. A new fan could be wired easily to the existing switch, which would operate both the fan and the light. But for a bathroom fan to be effective, it needs to remain running after the user has left the bathroom. By wiring the light and fan on separate switches, the light can be turned off to conserve energy while the fan clears moisture from the room. Better yet, an electronic timer switch (www.efi.org) turns on the fan and light together, but has an integral timer that keeps the fan running for up to an hour after the switch and light are turned off.

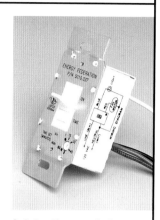

A delay-timer switch keeps the fan running until the steam clears.

WIRING THE FAN TO A DELAY-TIMER SWITCH
Although the neutrals can be spliced together and share a wire leading back to the switch box, separate power supplies are necessary for the light and fan to operate individually. A 14/3 wire, which you'll probably have to add, is ideal for this situation.

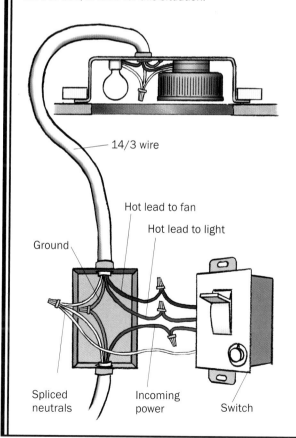

14/3 wire

Hot lead to fan

Hot lead to light

Ground

Spliced neutrals

Incoming power

Switch

Sealant, Blocking, and Screws Secure the Fan

Keeping moisture out of the attic is just as important as getting it out of the bathroom. Use blocking and screws to secure the fan and sealant to prevent air leakage.

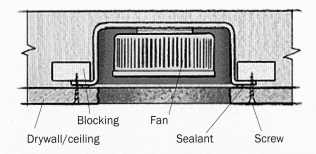

Blocking   Fan

Drywall/ceiling   Sealant   Screw

Set the fan on a bed of sealant. Create an airtight bond between the fan and the ceiling with a thick bead of sealant around the perimeter of the hole. Place the fan in the hole carefully, and make sure the flange sits flat on the ceiling and sealant.

Short, Straight Ductwork Vents Air Efficiently

When a curve is necessary, attach the duct to the fan, and create a short, sweeping arc toward the ceiling to determine the duct length as well as the best location for the roof vent. Trace around the duct's perimeter to make a mark for the vent location. After the exhaust duct is connected to the roof vent, wrap it with duct insulation to reduce the chance of condensation inside the duct in the winter and outside the duct in the summer.

A screw marks the spot on the roof. Drive a screw through the sheathing to mark the location on the roof where the vent hole will be cut.

Secure the fan from below. Anchor the fan to the ceiling with drywall screws. The screws will be hidden by the fan's cover and light.

Seal all ductwork tightly. Slip the duct all the way onto the fan's exhaust port, and seal it with duct tape. Use aluminum duct tape because the common fabric-backed kind deteriorates over time.

Install a Leak-Free Roof Vent

Don't Cut through Tabs

Trace the vent receptacle onto the roof around the screw. If the circle is touching a shingle's tabs, remove that shingle before cutting the hole.

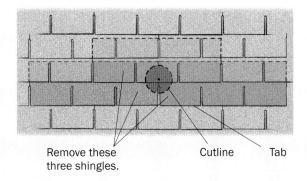

Remove these three shingles.　　Cutline　　Tab

Cut a hole large enough for the vent. The hole for the vent should be slightly larger than the duct receptacle to allow the ductwork coming from the fan to slide all the way onto the receptacle.

Flashing Prevents Water Leaks

Keep water out of the attic by flashing around three sides of the roof vent.

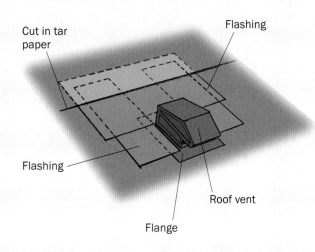

Cut in tar paper　　Flashing

Flashing

Roof vent

Flange

Both sides first. Slipped beneath the underlying tar paper and overlapping the flange, the flashing extends onto the shingle below.

The vent faces down the roof. Slip the vent into the hole with the opening facing down the slope of the roof, and secure it by driving a galvanized roofing nail at each corner.

Cut around the vent and replace the shingles. Before replacing the shingles, cut them to fit closely around the vent. Overlap the flange on the top and both sides.

Connect the duct. Back in the attic, connect the duct to the vent and seal it with aluminum duct tape.

Overlap everything. A third piece of flashing, which also slips under the tar paper, overlaps the flange and the side flashing.

Breathing Fresh Air into Bathroom Ventilation

■ BY SCOTT GIBSON

Bathroom fans have been around as long as their owners' reluctance to use them. Like a low-flying jet, early generations of bathroom fans were so loud they could rattle your teeth. So homeowners left them off, mirrors steamed up, and bathroom walls glistened with condensation.

In an older house without much insulation and with a row of drafty windows, the bathroom typically would dry before the bad stuff started—but not in a new house. Contemporary houses are built to be tight, with low-infiltration windows and walls packed with insulation that stops drafts cold. That's good news for your heating and cooling bills, but it's bad for unventilated bathrooms, which now are prone to mold, poor indoor-air quality, and structural damage from long-term moisture exposure.

The good news is that the latest bathroom exhaust fans are so quiet that you barely can hear them. Models include self-

Roof vent

Remote fan

Insulated duct

Intake grille with
integral light

Intake
grille

Timer
switch
controls
fan.

¾-in. gap for
makeup air

QUIET, POWERFUL, AND SOPHISTICATED
A single well-designed fan installation can solve
whole-house ventilation problems by removing
moisture from multiple sources.

Installation Guidelines

- With a remote fan, use soft, flexible duct for the first 5 ft. to reduce fan noise.
- Ducts in unconditioned spaces should be insulated to reduce condensation.
- For ceiling-mounted fans, choose galvanized steel or PVC ducts, which have less airflow resistance than flexible vinyl or aluminum.
- Install a UL-listed fan in a shower stall or over a tub, and put it on a circuit protected by a ground-fault circuit interrupter.
- Ceiling inlets are more effective than wall inlets at gathering heat and moisture.
- Always duct exhaust air outside, never into an attic or a basement.

contained units that mount in the ceiling or wall as well as remote units that mount some distance away from the bathroom and draw air from more than one inlet. In addition to features such as built-in lights and heaters, exhaust fans can be controlled by circuitry that cycles the blower on and off in response to humidity levels in the room. Choosing the right fan comes down to two considerations: how much noise the fan makes and how much air it moves.

Start by Choosing the Right Fan Size

For bathrooms up to 100 sq. ft. with an 8-ft. ceiling, an exhaust fan should move 1 cubic foot of air per minute (cfm) for each square foot of floor area. A 70-sq.-ft. bathroom, for example, requires a fan rated for no less than 70 cfm—enough to change the air in the room eight times an hour.

In bathrooms larger than 100 sq. ft., the fan-sizing rule is based on the number and the type of fixtures the unit will serve. Enclosed water closets, showers, and bathtubs each require 50 cfm of fan capacity, while a jetted tub needs 100 cfm. Separate exhaust outlets over each of the fixtures or a single exhaust point that handles the entire bathroom can provide ventilation. Exhaust intakes should be installed away from air-supply ducts, and bathroom doors should have a ¾-in. gap at the bottom so that makeup air can enter the room.

Fan-capacity recommendations assume the fan will move the amount of air that it's rated for, but that's not always the case. Manufacturers arrive at cfm ratings by testing fans against 0.1 in. of static pressure. This rating assumes a nearly ideal installation: a short, straight run of rigid duct and a cap that doesn't restrict airflow. If your installation requires a duct run longer than 12 ft., more than one elbow, or flexible duct, you should check the manufacturer's recommendations and increase the fan size accordingly.

Surface-Mounted Fans Serve a Single Exhaust Outlet

Ceiling-mounted fans are designed to draw air through a single port and exhaust it through a cap in the roof or wall. Installation is relatively simple because the fan and the grille are one unit. Capacities typically start at 50 cfm (the minimum required by code in a bathroom without an operable window) and range upward to about 400 cfm. Prices begin at about $100 for quiet, ENERGY STAR–rated models from manufacturers like Broan NuTone and Panasonic. Pricier models have built-in lights and infrared or electrical-resistance heaters.

Because warm, moisture-laden air collects at the ceiling, these fans expel it quickly. One disadvantage, though, is that ceiling

New Fans Are Efficient

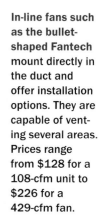

In-line fans such as the bullet-shaped Fantech mount directly in the duct and offer installation options. They are capable of venting several areas. Prices range from $128 for a 108-cfm unit to $226 for a 429-cfm fan.

Ceiling fans don't need big plastic grilles. Broan NuTone's combination recessed light/fan costs about $110. Different trim designs are available to blend in with traditional lighting (inset photo)

American Aldes multiport fans have a separate port for each duct run. This model, with two 50-cfm ports and a larger port capable of 100 cfm, lists for $385.

New-generation fans, like this NuTone QTXEN 80-cfm model, operate more quietly than a kitchen refrigerator, a noise threshold described as 1 sone. Street price: about $175.

Perfect for first-floor bathrooms, the fan on this Fantech unit mounts on a house's exterior to reduce noise and ease installation. Street price: $165.

A Roar Or a Whisper?

Noise levels for ceiling- and wall-mounted fans are described in sones. Unlike the more familiar decibel scale, the sone scale is linear: A 2-sone fan makes twice as much noise as a 1-sone fan.

The Home Ventilating Institute (www.hvi.org), an industry trade group, conducts standardized tests for bathroom fans. Older fans or inexpensive models can reach 4 sones. Yet one of the new Broan NuTone models and several Panasonic models are rated at less than 0.3 sones.

Noise levels, however, increase with fan capacity. For example, Panasonic's 80-cfm WhisperCeiling™ model is rated at 0.3 sones, while its 290-cfm model has more than three times the flow but also produces 2 sones of sound.

Sone ratings don't apply to remote-mounted fans because there are too many installation variables at work.

fans can't pick up exhaust air from more than one point. Bathrooms with separate water closets need an additional unit, and in large bathrooms, a high-capacity fan has to draw exhaust air relatively long distances. Bigger fans mean more noise and a larger grille in the ceiling. To mask the appearance of ceiling fans, Broan NuTone has developed a recessed light/fan combination with trims designed to match those of conventional recessed lights.

Wall-mounted fans are another option. Although they can be easier to install than a ceiling unit when remodeling, through-the-wall units typically generate more noise than ceiling units and also admit more noise from outside. Moreover, drawing air from the wall instead of the ceiling is not as efficient. As a result, manufacturers generally don't suggest wall-mounted fans as a first choice.

Remote Fans Can Handle Multiple Pickup Points

In large bathrooms or ones with separate water closets, remote fans have one big advantage: They can pull air from several grilles in different parts of the room or even from adjacent bathrooms. Fan motors can be as far as 50 ft. from the grille, reducing noise.

Several types are available. Cylindrical in-line fans, such as those made by Fantech and Continental, are mounted in the duct. In a bathroom with two or more pickup points, connections are made in the duct before it reaches the fan housing. Rectangular multiport models, such as those from American Aldes, have a separate port for each length of duct. Other types of remote fans are installed against an outside wall.

Intake grilles on remote-fan systems are much smaller than ceiling-mounted fixtures, and versions with integral lights are available. Grilles can be installed in a shower or over a sink to collect moisture close to its source. With most models, serving more than one pickup point with a single fan means that all pickup points are either on or off. However, American Aldes's VentZone Systems® allow you to connect up to eight rooms to a single fan but turn on only individual pickup points.

The Right Switch Improves Fan Performance

Bathroom exhaust fans often are less effective than they could be because they are turned off too soon. If a fan is switched off right after a shower, most of the moisture is still in the room, clinging to the ceiling and the shower walls and trapped in damp towels. Expelling moisture actually can take 20 minutes to 30 minutes.

A variety of switches allow fans to run longer, or to cycle on and off automatically

Switches Make Them Smarter

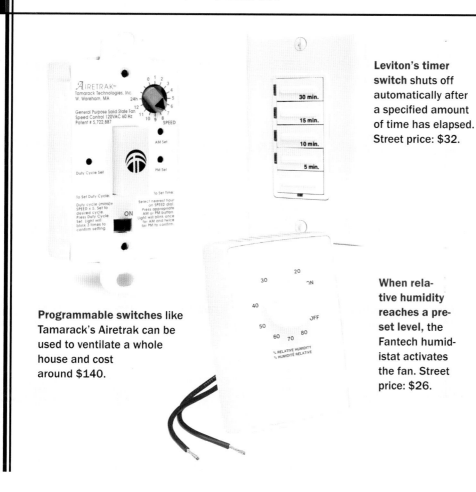

Leviton's timer switch shuts off automatically after a specified amount of time has elapsed. Street price: $32.

Programmable switches like Tamarack's Airetrak can be used to ventilate a whole house and cost around $140.

When relative humidity reaches a preset level, the Fantech humidistat activates the fan. Street price: $26.

American Aldes
800-255-7749
www.americanaldes.com

Broan NuTone
800-548-0790
www.broan-nutone.com

Continental Fan
Manufacturing
800-779-4021
www.continentalfan.com

Energy Federation
800-379-4121
www.efi.org

Fantech
800-747-1762
www.fantech.net

Leviton
800-824-3005
www.leviton.com

Panasonic
866-292-7292
www.panasonic.com

Tamarack Technologies
800-222-5932
www.tamtech.com

Sensors inside each port ensure that each pickup point of this American Aldes fan operates at its rated cfm.

as they are needed. The simplest type is an electronic or mechanical timer programmed to keep the fan running for a set amount of time. Leviton's version lets you select the running time with the push of a button. A variation is Energy Federation's delay-off switch, which keeps the fan on after the switch is turned off. An adjustment screw behind the cover plate allows users to set the extended run time.

Automatic controls, such as Tamarack's Airetrak®, are more sophisticated, allowing a fan to be programmed to cycle on and off throughout the day. These controls are especially useful when the bathroom fan (typically a large remote fan) is used for whole-house ventilation to provide the 0.35 air changes per hour recommended by the American Society of Heating, Refrigerating and Air-

Conditioning Engineers. A boost feature on some models temporarily increases fan speed when the shower or bathtub is used.

Humidity-sensing switches turn on a fan whenever relative humidity reaches a preset level. An override switch allows the fan to be turned on regardless of humidity.

Finally, motion detectors can be used to power up a fan as soon as anyone enters the bathroom, then turn it off after they leave.

Scott Gibson is a contributing editor for Fine Homebuilding.

Fight Mold with Paperless Drywall

■ BY MYRON R. FERGUSON

Paperless Product Choices.
Paper-faced mold-resistant
drywall panels are made by
most gypsum companies,
but only a few make paperless
gypsum for interior applications.
The average cost for a $\frac{1}{2}$-in.-
thick 4×8 sheet is about $18,
but thicker panels and different
sizes are also available from
each company.

- Aqua-Tough™
  www.usg.com
- DensArmor® Plus
  www.gp.com
- GreenGlass®
  www.templeinland.com

Let's face it—there's been a lot of talk about mold in the past few years. The topic has gotten plenty of attention in the news, has been the focus of lots of building-science research, and has made many home-owners nervous. Here's the thing: Mold spores are everywhere and are nearly impossible to avoid, never mind eliminate. What we can do, though, is help to prevent those mold spores from taking root in our indoor living spaces. That's where products like paperless drywall come into play.

Mold needs four things to grow: oxygen, water, a temperature between 40°F and 100°F, and an organic food source. Considering this group of ingredients, it's not surprising that mold is commonly found on lumber in the basement, on the wall behind the sink in the kitchen, and on the wallpaper adhesive in the bathroom.

The first step in preventing mold growth is to get firm control over the level of moisture in the air (see "Breathing Fresh Air Into Bathroom Ventilation" on p. 192). After that, the focus should be on eliminating the organic food source.

Back Up Screws with Adhesive

Paperless drywall can be fastened with ordinary drywall screws. I use 1¼-in. screws for both ½-in. and ⅝-in. panels. Because these panels are harder to fasten properly, I don't rely on screws alone.

Adhesive is cheap insurance. Applying a bead of drywall adhesive not only reduces the number of fasteners necessary on wall panels (see the chart on the facing page), but it also makes up for the high likelihood that some of the fasteners will be set too deep. Without the paper facing, it's much easier to overdrive fasteners into fiberglass-faced products. Make sure to adjust the clutch of the screw gun so that fasteners are driven until they indent the surface of the board slightly, but not so far that they tear through and lose holding power. Consider adhesive and screws to be best practice with fiberglass-faced products.

I often leave screws slightly proud and then sink them by hand for a perfect dimpled depth.

Glue Means Fewer Screws

There are several brands of drywall adhesive on the market, but any construction adhesive that meets ASTM C-557 can be used. If the local building inspector wants to see the proper amount of fasteners and can't verify what's behind the walls, consider the belt-and-suspenders approach: adhesive and standard screw spacing. See the chart below to compare fastening schedules with and without adhesive.

Framing	Walls	Walls with adhesive	Ceilings	Ceilings with adhesive
16 in. o.c.	Every 16 in.	Every 24 in.	Every 12 in.	Every 16 in.
24 in. o.c.	Every 12 in.	Every 24 in.*	Every 12 in.	Every 16 in.

* Every 16 in. if the wall is load-bearing

Paper Is a Gourmet Meal for Mold

Because mold decomposes organic (once living) material as a food source, the paper facings on the front and back of drywall are an easy target. Most drywall manufacturers have fought this problem by offering modern versions of the old wax-coated greenboard that has been used in bathrooms for years. Many of these modern paper-faced products even scored a perfect 10 on the ASTM standard for mold resistance. For the ultimate peace of mind, though, a few drywall manufacturers have now created paperless drywall, removing all sources of organic food (see "Paperless Product Choices" on p. 198).

By replacing drywall's paper facing with an inorganic fiberglass mat, products like DensArmor Plus (shown in this installation) offer excellent mold resistance compared to standard paper-faced wallboard products. But don't get a false sense of security; these products are only as good as the installation.

For example, I once had a truckload of paperless drywall delivered to a job site, and when I started to install the product, I noticed that the back side of one sheet was dirty. I guess the drywall must have been stacked at a convenient height for a lunch or a coffee break because somebody had spilled coffee or soda on it. Then dirt and sawdust from the lumberyard and the job site clung to the sheet. If I hadn't noticed the stain and tossed the sheet, I would have quickly defeated the mold resistance of the paperless drywall. If paperless drywall isn't handled properly or installed correctly, the job may be little more than a pricier route to the same place.

Paperless products behave similarly to standard paper-faced drywall, but they are a bit more fragile to handle and install, require different products to tape, and typically must be finished to a more uniform surface before being painted. Learn these quirks, though, and you're likely to have a successful experience with paperless products.

Myron R. Ferguson (www.thatdrywallguy.com) is a drywall contractor in Galway, New York.

Put Away Power Tools to Minimize Dust

Because paperless drywall has fiberglass facings on the front and back, it's in your best interest to keep airborne dust to a minimum. I recommend wearing a dust mask when cutting these products. Drywall dust alone warrants a mask. Add fiberglass to the equation, and your throat and lungs can become seriously irritated. Also, gloves and a long-sleeve shirt will help you to avoid getting itchy slivers of fiberglass on your hands and arms.

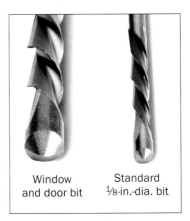

Avoid the router where possible. Drywall routers are a fast method for making drywall cutouts. In fact, they leave an even cleaner cut in paperless drywall than in regular paper-faced products. However, they create an enormous amount of fiberglass-laden dust. For cutting around electrical boxes, the small amount of dust is a fair trade-off for the more accurate cutout, but for door and window openings, use a utility knife and a handsaw.

Large offcuts falling to the floor can kick up lots of dust. To avoid this, leave a little bit of drywall at the edge of the cut, then slice the piece free with a utility knife and carefully remove it.

Window and door bit

Standard ⅛-in.-dia. bit

If you use a router, use it smart. If you can't bring yourself to part with the drywall router, there are still ways to minimize the dust. Begin by avoiding the larger ¼-in.-dia. "window and door" drywall bits. Bigger bits can be pushed harder and faster and are less likely to break, but they also create much more dust than the standard ⅛-in.-dia. bits.

New Work Habit #3

Switch to Inorganic Tape

Paper tape set in premixed joint compound is a manufacturer-approved option for finishing joints on paperless drywall, but most encourage the use of setting-type compound (top right photo) and mesh tape, which further reduces the chances of mold growth by removing a food source. Standard mesh tape is widely available and a fine choice, but I prefer FibaFuse® fiberglass tape; www.sgtf.com (top left photo), which has a thinner open-fiber weave. Either way, these tapes come with their own set of rules.

Embed the tape with care. Apply the mesh tape in a thinned mixture of compound because it's easy to cut through fiberglass tape accidentally with the edge of a taping knife. Likewise, use a corner knife to avoid tears on inside corners, a relatively new knife for the rest of the seams, and fairly gentle handling all around.

TIP

Use a relatively new taping knife for working with mesh tape. The older the knife, the sharper the edges will be.

New Work Habit #4

Sand Where You Can; Skim-Coat Where You Can't

Fiberglass-faced wallboard has a slightly rougher surface than paper-faced drywall, and there's a lot of fuss about how to make this surface blend with the smooth-sanded taped seams. A typical drywall job is taken to what's known as a level-4 finish: two coats of joint compound on all seams. Paperless drywall can be finished to the same level, but only if you plan to roll on a high-solids primer. It's not much extra work either to sand all the walls lightly to knock down the fiberglass texture or to do a level-5 finish (two coats of joint compound on all seams, followed by a skim coat of the entire surface).

OPTION 1

Lightly sand the walls and ceilings after applying the third coat of joint compound to the seams. Unlike paper-faced drywall, these products become smoother when sanded. The trade-off to this faster approach is more airborne fiberglass dust, so protect yourself accordingly.

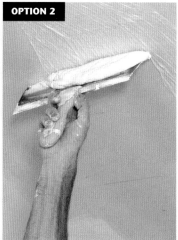

OPTION 2

Skim-coating the entire surface of the drywall with a thin layer of joint compound is fine if you're comfortable with taping knives. In fact, this is the best option for any type of drywall that will be coated with high-sheen paint or exposed to strong raking light at any point in the day.

Cheaper Hot Water

■ BY DAVE YATES

As a mechanical contractor, I've been responding to homeowners' concerns about high energy bills for a long time. When fuel costs escalate, these calls become more frequent, and more urgent.

Heating water for domestic purposes—showers, laundry, dishes, and the rest—accounts for 12 percent to 26 percent of a home's energy use. That's between $240 and $520 for an average U.S. household. But you can put your hot-water system on an energy diet without sacrificing comfort. The six strategies that follow range widely in cost and complexity, but all will reduce your energy bills and your carbon footprint.

Dave Yates owns and operates F.W. Behler Inc., a mechanical-contracting firm in York, Pennsylvania.

1. Insulate Your Water Heater

The facts: If your tank-style water heater predates the 2004 federally mandated increase in tank insulation, it's costing you money every day in standby heat losses.

The fix: Adding an insulating jacket costs less than $30 and takes less than an hour. If you have a gas- or oil-fired water heater, follow the jacket's instructions carefully to avoid cutting off combustion air or interfering with exhaust. All appliances using fossil fuels produce deadly carbon monoxide (CO) during combustion. The combustion-air intake and exhaust draft are two components that keep CO in check. If either is compromised, dangerous levels of CO can leak into the home.

When insulating electric water heaters, be sure to allow access to the elements and the wiring inlet for future service. The inlet/outlet should be accessible for routine inspection (leaks), and the temperature and pressure (T&P) relief valve should remain exposed with its drip leg extended within 6 in. of the floor for annual testing and for observation of any water discharge.

The savings: Wrapping an older water heater with an insulation kit can cut standby heat losses by 25 percent to 45 percent, saving you 5 percent to 10 percent on your water-heating costs.

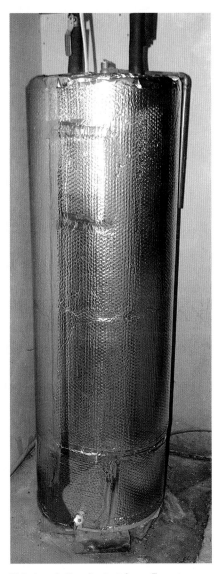

This insulation jacket from Energy Efficient Solutions (www.energy-efficientsolutions.com) has an R-6 value and fits most tanks up to 80 gal.

Diving into Dollars

Whenever there's waste in a home, it's only natural to want to know the cost of that waste in real dollars. That's not too hard to calculate on a specific job when I have all the facts: the type of fuel used, the efficiency of the water-heating system, the length and other characteristics of the pipe runs, and the amount of temperature rise required (the difference between the temperature of the water when it enters the home and the temperature at which the water heater is set). Likewise, when I'm examining a specific house, I can fill in the blank on another big variable: the price the homeowners pay for fuel, which varies nationally and fluctuates constantly.

With so many variables, though, it's tough to make generalizations about exactly how much savings will result from a given water-system improvement. In most cases in this article, I offer potential savings as a percentage of energy conserved. In some cases, I use specific examples where I spell out the variables to arrive at a meaningful dollar-savings figure. But as they say in the car business, your individual mileage may vary.

Your local mechanical-systems specialist, plumber, or energy consultant can help you determine more specifically the savings you can expect from any water-system improvements in your home.

2. Insulate Your Home's Hot-Water Pipes

The facts: Every foot of bare ½-in. copper tubing carrying 120°F water around a 70°F home loses 14.1 Btu an hour; ¾-in. tubing loses 19.1 Btu per hour (1 Btu is the amount of energy needed to raise the temperature of 1 lb. of water by 1°F). You can substantially reduce this loss by insulating the hot-water supply lines.

The fix: Pipe insulation comes in 6-ft. strips and is typically fiberglass or foam-based material. Choose the best you can afford; fiberglass or elastomeric foam will save you more than cheaper foam tubing.

Insulation should fit snugly over the tubing to prevent condensation, and all joints and slits should be firmly sealed. Foam pipe insulation is often available with a preglued slit; you can use contact cement to seal butt ends or mitered joints. Some cements require adequate ventilation, so read and follow all instructions. Fiberglass insulation should be handled according to manufacturers' instructions. (Always wear safety glasses when working with fiber-

glass.) Costs range from under $2 per 6-ft. length for R-2 insulation to $12 per length for R-8 UV-resistant Armaflex®, used to insulate exterior piping in solar systems.

In a retrofit, the amount of piping accessible for insulating depends on the home's style. The main distribution lines in most houses are accessible through the basement; only the risers in the walls can't be accessed. In one-story homes, then, this means you can insulate all but a few final feet of piping.

The savings: If three family members shower for 20 minutes a day each, with hot water traveling 50 ft. through uninsulated ¾-in. pipe from the heater to the shower, the daily energy loss adds up to 975 Btu. Insulate that same run of piping with 1-in. fiberglass, and the energy loss is reduced to just 233 Btu. (That's like not having to heat almost 542 gal. of water a year.) By insulating the pipes, the family above saves about $12 a year if their water heater is gas-fired and $23 a year if it burns oil.

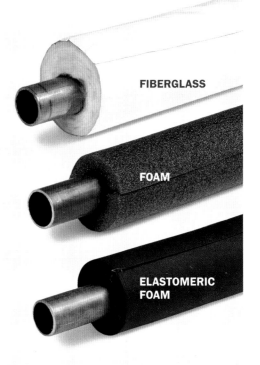

FIBERGLASS

FOAM

ELASTOMERIC FOAM

Choose the best insulation

All pipe insulation is not equal. The chart at right shows the varying effectiveness of insulation types applied to a 50-ft. run of ¾-in. copper hot-water pipe. The effectiveness is measured in Btu lost over one hour, the total amount of time the shower was used by the family cited in the example above.

Insulation Type	Btu Lost
No insulation (bare copper)	975
⅜-in. foam	425
½-in. foam	366
½-in. fiberglass	325
¾-in. foam	301
1-in. fiberglass	**233**

Source: Based on data from www.engineeringtoolbox.com

3. Find and Repair Leaks and Drips

The facts: Leaky plumbing that's not causing damage—such as a faucet dripping into a sink—is often ignored. But a single hot-water faucet that drips once a second (60 drips per minute) costs a homeowner with a gas-fired water heater $22 a year in wasted Btu alone. Depending on where you live, you might also pay for water and its disposal; at my house, that adds about $24. Not bad? If that leak is actually a dribble that fills one 8-oz. cup a minute, it'll cost $348 annually—plus $230 for the water and its disposal. If your water heater runs on electricity or oil, these numbers will be even higher.

The fix: Most leak repairs are manageable for any handy homeowner and can be done with little expense. Leaks in more remote areas can easily go undetected, but many can be found with a little investigation.

If you have municipal water, the meter probably has a tattletale spinner; if the faucets are all shut off and it's spinning, you've got a leak. If the meter doesn't have a tattletale gauge, record the reading in the evening after your last use and again in the morning before using any water. If there's a difference, then you have a leak.

Well-water systems present a different challenge for detecting leaks. In this case, a pressure gauge like the Watts® IWTG can be screwed onto any available

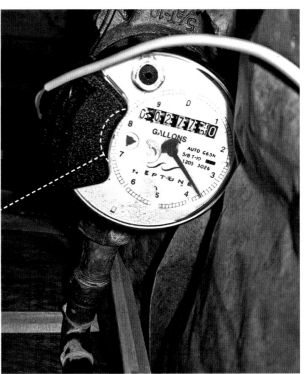

The small red triangle on this water meter is a tattletale gauge. If it's spinning when all faucets are shut off, you have a leak.

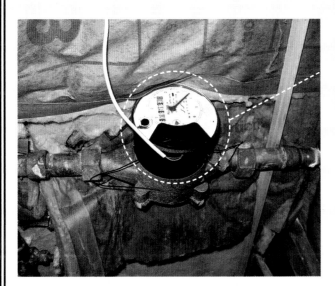

hose-thread faucet. Open the faucet, return to the well tank, and close the outlet valve. This isolates the home's piping from the well tank. Water is essentially noncompressible, so even a minute leak—like a slow drip—will show up on the gauge as a decrease in pressure.

Other areas to check visually for leaking hot water include the water heater's inlet, outlet, boiler drain, and relief-valve ports, where leaks can be wicked into surrounding insulation and evaporated quickly by the heated storage tank. Other common leakage sites include pinholes in piping; joints that weep where solder has cracked or where threads are not adequately tightened; and joints between different types of piping.

Once you've found the leak, the first step— whether you tackle the repairs yourself or call in a pro—is shutting off the water (something everyone in your household should know in case of a plumbing emergency). Next, you have to determine what you need to repair the leak. Pipe and joint leaks can be sealed with do-it-yourself kits sold at home centers; the kits contain a wide variety of push-on self-sealing fittings or compression fittings that adapt to virtually any type of piping. You might want to call in a pro if soldering or special tools (PEX crimp ring or expander tools) are required.

If a faucet or toilet is leaking and you're tackling the repairs yourself, I suggest you first search the Internet for your toilet or faucet model. You're likely to find an exploded parts view along with details about repairs or parts to

A Watts gauge helps to detect leaks in well systems. For testing, screw it onto a laundry spigot or any hose-thread faucet.

order. Armed with this information, a trip to your local big-box retailer won't be half as frustrating as it would be if you were to stare blindly at a wall lined with thousands of parts. Once you have the parts, complete the replacement according to the manufacturer's directions.

The savings: Let's say you've discovered several drippy faucets. You check the water-meter reading over an 8-hour period and find you've lost 4 gal. (that's 126 drips per minute). Is it worth your time and effort to fix the faucets? Repair parts might cost $5 to $50 and a few hours of your time. If the leaks are on the hot side and you heat with oil, those drips cost about $185 a year. Chances are the repairs will last for 10 years (or longer), saving you $1845 over the long run.

4. Add a Thermal-Expansion Tank

The facts: When water is heated, it expands. Heating 40 gal. of 40°F water to 140°F generates ¾ gal. of thermal expansion. Without an expansion tank, this water leaks out of the tank's temperature and pressure (T&P) valve, ruins the water heater, or causes a leak in the piping—the weakest link in the chain. T&P relief valves discharge under three conditions: pressure that is 150 psi (pounds per square inch) or above; temperatures above 210°F; or when the valve is worn out or fouled with debris. A badly leaking relief valve can double or triple your water-heating bill.

The fix: A properly sized thermal-expansion tank (TXT) should be installed to accommodate the increase in volume as water is heated. You'll find TXTs in home centers next to the water heaters. Installation instructions come with each tank.

Grip fittings available today have virtually eliminated the need to solder piping, so the trickiest part of installing a TXT is providing proper support. Because water weighs 8.34 lb. per gal., good support is essential to prevent stressing newly installed joints. Provide that support with metal hanger strap-

ping; don't use the cheap plastic stuff. Most thermal-expansion tanks for residential use come in two sizes: 2-gal. and 4.5-gal. For an extra $15, your system will be better protected by the larger one.

The savings: Adding a properly sized TXT can save money by reducing wear and tear on your home's plumbing. The water heater will last longer; the faucets won't wear out as quickly; and piping and fittings won't break, split, or develop leaks caused by high pressure. It's a wise investment.

THERMAL-EXPANSION TANK
As water is heated, it expands. A properly sized TXT gives the expanding volume of water a place to grow while protecting the tank and plumbing system from thermal-expansion stresses. Water cannot be compressed, but air can. The two are separated by the rubber diaphragm inside the expansion tank.

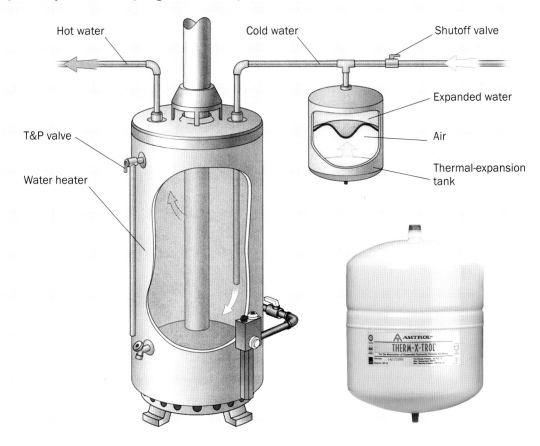

Hot water · Cold water · Shutoff valve · Expanded water · Air · Thermal-expansion tank · T&P valve · Water heater

5. Add a Gravity-Fed Recirculation System

The facts: A family of four wastes as much as 12,000 gal. of water every year waiting for hot water to travel from the heater to the tap. That wait wastes water and energy, and puts an unnecessary burden on sewage-treatment systems.

The fix: Recirculating systems eliminate the wait by delivering instant hot water to all the fixtures in your house. Most systems use an electric pump, but even energy-efficient pumps cost money to run. You can put the pump on a switch, timer, or motion sensor for efficiency, but you sacrifice the convenience of hot water on demand.

If you really want to save energy dollars and always have hot water at the tap, ask your plumber about a gravity-fed recirculation system. If you want to reduce your water-heating bill to $0, consider combining gravity-fed recirculation with a solar water heater, as I did in my home.

This is how gravity-fed recirculation works: When water is heated, its molecules expand and become less dense. Gravity causes the denser, and therefore heavier, cold-water molecules to sink to the lowest point in the system. All that's needed to set up circulation between the hotter water at the top and the colder water at the bottom is a loop that returns from wherever the desire for instant hot water is located to the lower connection of the water heater. This generates a thermal circulation flow that gently moves hot water out to the end of the loop and back through the return. The entire loop must be well insulated to prevent wasting energy and short-cycling. With no moving parts to wear out, this system supplies instant hot water throughout the house 24 hours a day.

The savings: At between $600 and $1400, the initial cost of a recirculation system might seem like a deal breaker, but if you consider the return on investment (rather than payback), you'll see the real value a recirculation system can offer. Let's say you're wasting 12,000 gal. a year waiting for hot water to come through. Eliminating that waste with a gravity-fed recirculation system saves you $265 in water, sewage, and water-heating costs (in my case, roughly half that expense was for heating the water). Now, if you're saving a total of $265 annually and the system costs $1200, the annual ROI is an attractive 22 percent. A hefty tax-free return and no waiting for hot water—it doesn't get better than that. A recirculation system powered by a pump will save you somewhat less.

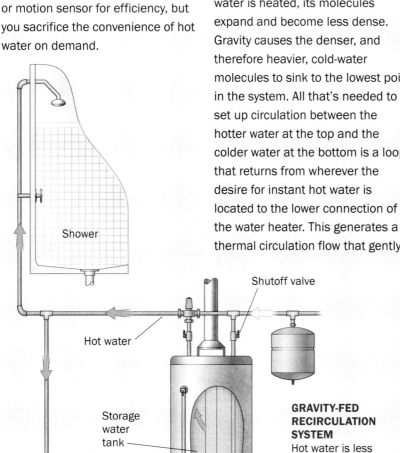

Shower

Shutoff valve

Hot water

Storage water tank

Check valve

GRAVITY-FED RECIRCULATION SYSTEM
Hot water is less dense than cold water and flows gently outward to the point where the return is connected. As the water cools, it "falls" downward by gravity and back into the tank.

6. Toss Your Old Tank and Try Some New Technology

The facts: Efficiencies for water-heating systems range from 63 percent to 99 percent, and savings rise markedly with these efficiencies. Because upgrading your water heater can save significantly on energy costs, start by evaluating its efficiency. To the right is a list of household water-heating systems from least to most efficient based on the energy factor (EF), a measure of overall efficiency. Energy efficiency is not the same as cost efficiency, however. Electric storage-tank heaters have a high EF, yet typically cost more to operate; the wiser economic choice would be an appliance with a lower fuel cost, even if it's a bit less efficient. Also, while all indirect water heaters are highly efficient, their actual efficiency depends on the boiler they're connected to.

Least Efficiency Most

- Oil storage tank
- Propane-gas storage tank; natural-gas storage tank
- Propane-gas tankless; natural-gas tankless
- Electric storage tank
- Electric tankless
- Indirect water heaters attached to electric, oil, or gas boilers
- Tank-style heat-pump water heater
- Navien natural-gas 98 percent efficiency tankless water heater
- Solar

The fix: Try a new tank. Replacing a tank-style water heater is a relatively straightforward task. Due to federally mandated changes, today's models are safer and more efficient than those from just a few years ago. One change is beefier insulation (making them slightly bigger, so measure the space first). The feds have also lowered the Btu input, which, while boosting efficiency, also lowers the water heater's gallon-per-hour recovery rate. As a result, you might need to increase storage volume by installing, for example, a 50-gal. model in place of a 40-gal. one.

You can expect to spend $500 to $1900 for a good-quality water heater. The range is due to the variety of gas and oil tank-style water heaters available today: atmospheric chimney-vented, where exhaust exits unassisted through a chimney (the least expensive to purchase, but the most expensive to operate); indirect-vented, where an electric blower exhausts combustion gases through horizontal piping (moderately more expensive to purchase and more demanding to install correctly); and high-efficiency sealed-combustion models with direct vents, in which both exhaust and combustion air are hard-piped to and from the home's exterior (the most expensive, but the least costly to operate). Sealed combustion also eliminates combustion-related outdoor-air infiltration, which adds to a home's heating load.

The savings: Switching out an old tank style with 63 percent efficiency for another with 67 percent efficiency won't save you much, but upgrading to a 90 percent efficient, sealed-combustion model is a step in the right direction.

This Navien tankless water heater has an overall efficiency of 98 percent.

The fix: Go tankless. Navien broke new ground when they introduced a 98 percent efficiency model. Compare that to a tank-style chimney-vented gas water heater with a 63 percent efficiency (averaged over 24 hours and including stand-by energy lost) and there's a potential to save 35 percent in annual operating costs—providing you continue to use the same amount of hot water. But here's the catch: Because there's no threat of running out of hot water with a tankless heater, some people who've installed them start using more hot water, wiping out any savings. Used with restraint, however, tankless models will save money.

The savings: Many of my customers switch from tank to tankless for the endless supply of hot water, rather than the cost savings. The cost of replacing a tank-style water heater with a tankless model ranges from $1,500 to $2,900 (after the tax credit), about $650 to $1,950 more than you could expect to spend to install a tank-style gas water heater. If you control your hot-water use and get the maximum 35% savings, you'll save about $132 on a typical annual water-heating bill of $400.

The fix: Heat pump water heaters. Tank-style water heaters that incorporate an on-board heat-pump offer direct drop-in replacements for standard tank-style electric water heaters. They yield substantial savings if programmed and sized correctly to operate in their most-efficient mode using the compressor. EF ratings average 2.5, meaning, in plain English, that for every $1.00 you spend for electricity, you get $2.50 of heated water.

The savings: Installed costs will range from $1,950 to $2,950 (after the tax credit)—about $1,000 more than you could expect to spend to install an old-style electric water heater of equal size. You can expect savings of about $252 on a typical water-heating bill of $400.

The fix: Use your boiler. If you have a boiler for hydronic (water-based) heating, you can add an indirect water heater, essentially a tank that stores potable water heated through the boiler. Installed properly, an indirect water heater's operating efficiency will closely match the boiler's; when used with a high-efficiency modulating condensing boiler, the overall efficiency can range well above 90 percent. Because the boiler's full Btu output is devoted to making domestic hot water, these models can meet the output of tankless water heaters. With no need for fuel lines or flues, highly insulated indirect water tanks can be located remotely from their energy source (the boiler) and closer to the points of use, reducing the wait for hot water. Adding an indirect water heater to a hydronic-heating system costs $1600 to $2800. These units last up to 30 years and in life-cycle cost comparisons offer one of the lowest-overall costs for domestic hot water.

The savings: An indirect water heater is as efficient as the boiler to which it's connected, from 78 percent to 98 percent. The range of savings is just as broad: Depending on water usage, fuel type, and other factors, you could save from about $50 to $400 a year.

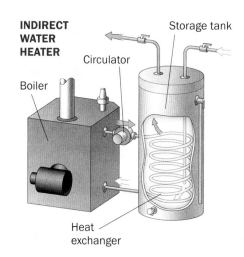

INDIRECT WATER HEATER — Boiler, Circulator, Storage tank, Heat exchanger

---

Liquid sunshine. The author assembles the Viessmann vacuum-tube solar array that produces 80 percent of the hot water for his home.

The fix: Get stoked by the sun. Solar hot-water systems provide free hot water, but at an up-front cost that might seem too steep: $6000 to $12,000, on average. Maybe that's why the minute solar is mentioned, everyone asks about the payback. Federal and local incentives can help offset the cost. (Visit the North Carolina Solar Center's database at www.dsireusa.org for incentives in your area.) Currently, the federal residential tax incentive for solar installations equals 30 percent of the system's cost. Solar hot-water systems fall into two categories: flat panel and vacuum tube. Both systems work well when properly installed and can last 30 years or longer.

The savings: My home's Viessmann® 30-vacuum-tube system produces about 80 percent of our hot-water needs (typical savings are 70 percent to 80 percent). My payback is expected to be 12 years, but my ROI at today's energy costs is 5 percent— better than current CD rates. As fuel costs increase, so does my ROI, which also shortens the payback time. Showering in liquid sunshine feels better, too.

Installing an Electric Radiant Floor

■ BY TOM MEEHAN

In my 35-plus years as a tile installer, I think the greatest improvement to tile floors is electric radiant heat. That warm feeling under your feet is something you will never take for granted, and it doesn't take much energy to operate an electric radiant floor. It can be as little as the energy it takes to run a 100w bulb. (Keep in mind that this is a comfort system, not the primary heat source for a room.)

Several types of electric radiant heat are on the market (see "Sources" on p. 218). Each electric radiant system has advantages, but they all have one thing in common: Like an electric blanket, they use a matrix of wires to conduct heat. For the remodeling project shown here, I used a NuHeat™ Mat (www.nuheat.com). This system consists of a mat made of a woven polyester fabric in which heat wires are embedded (see the drawing on p. 217). The mat is laminated to the subfloor with a layer of thinset, a special type of mortar that is used to adhere tile in areas that are exposed to moisture.

Heat Only the Areas That Are Walked On

First, determine how big a mat you need. If it's an open floor plan, measure the rectangular or square area that needs to be heated for an easy, off-the-shelf purchase. For complex installations, a detailed drawing submitted with a special order should include the location for the electrical hookup and the thermostatic controls. The manufacturer will configure a custom-fit system for your room. But remember that custom mats cost more than off-the-shelf ones and that you really need the wires only in the locations where you're likely to stand. In either case, heat wires should never run under a cabinet or toilet, where the wires can overheat and possibly burn out.

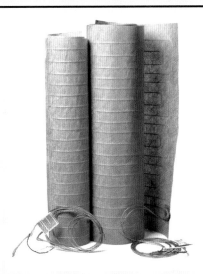

- Comes in numerous standard sizes
- Inexpensive to operate
- Heats only the area you want heated
- Custom mats are available
- Can be installed over most existing floors
- Thin enough so that it won't adversely affect floor height

Electric Radiant Heat Can Go over Existing Materials

The remodeling job illustrated here takes a different kind of preparation than new construction. A few years ago, I would have ripped out the old floor, right down to the subfloor. Now, I save the mess and extra cost, and install over a properly prepared vinyl floor.

The work starts with the electrician drilling a hole for the wires in an inconspicuous spot that doesn't see much traffic (see photo 1 on p. 218) or making a hole in the wall where the baseboard will cover it. Next, I scarify the vinyl with a grinder or sander to give the thinset a surface it can bond to (see photo 2 on p. 219). Then I nail off the floor with galvanized roofing nails 8 in. apart as if it were a piece of underlayment. This step ensures that no voids or inherent weak spots are in the floor. After nailing it off, I know this floor isn't going anywhere.

Installing the Heat Mat Is Not Difficult

Before I spread any thinset, I roll out the mat to make sure it fits. Knowing that the mat is working properly, I begin spreading a high-performance latex-modified thinset with a ¼-in. notched trowel (see photo 3 on p. 219). A high-performance thinset means

Anatomy of an Electric Radiant Floor

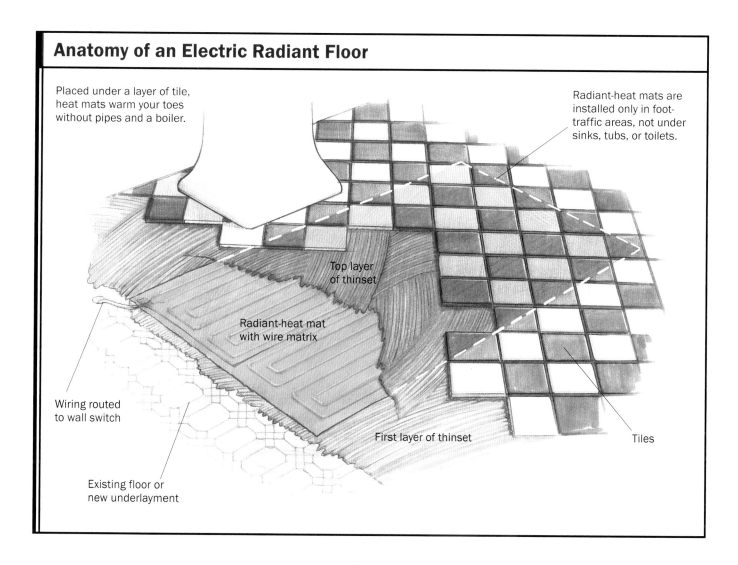

Placed under a layer of tile, heat mats warm your toes without pipes and a boiler.

Radiant-heat mats are installed only in foot-traffic areas, not under sinks, tubs, or toilets.

Top layer of thinset

Radiant-heat mat with wire matrix

Wiring routed to wall switch

First layer of thinset

Tiles

Existing floor or new underlayment

it can adhere to more resilient surfaces like vinyl because it has more polymers than other thinsets. Once the floor is coated, I can unroll the mat into the thinset (see photo 4 on p. 219).

Before and after installation, I connect the mat to a typical multimeter, which can be bought at Sears® for about $30, to check for any damage to the wires. SunTouch®, another electric-radiant-mat manufacturer, has a terrific proprietary alarm system called the LoudMouth™. If a wire is damaged during installation, the alarm sounds, and I know exactly where the problem is. Then I can have an electrician troubleshoot and repair any damage.

I work the mat forward, pushing it into the thinset. The wires are fragile and must be treated carefully. After the mat is spread out, I use a clean wood float to push it tight

while getting rid of any voids or air pockets (see photo 5 on p. 218). I start from the middle of the mat and work my way out.

When the mat is set, the electrician lays the thermostat sensor between the heat wires (see photo 6 on p. 219). The sensor can't cross any heating wires, or it won't accurately record floor temperature. Next, he feeds the wires down the hole he drilled earlier and completes the connections.

Protect the Mat When Setting the Tile

My main concern now is protecting the heat mat from being damaged as I install the tile. By simply placing heavy cardboard wherever I work or step, I'm able to place the tile safely. I begin with a skim coat of

Sources

EasyHeat®
800-537-4732
www.easyheat.com

Infloor® Radiant Heat
800-588-4470
www.infloor.com

NuHeat
800-778-9276
www.nuheat.com

STEP Warmfloor™
877-783-7832
ww.warmfloor.com

SunTouch
888-432-8932
www.suntouch.net

Warmly Yours
800-875-5285
www.warmlyyours.com

Test the Wires

Before installing the mat, check its integrity with a multimeter (volt/ohm meter) to detect any short circuits (top photo below). Because mat damage generally is caused with the trowel, it's important to check the mat throughout installation. The LoudMouth (bottom photo below) from SunTouch is a proprietary alarm that will sound if a short occurs during installation.

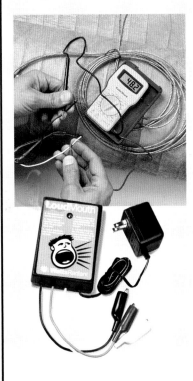

thinset using the flat side of a trowel to permeate the fabric of the heat mat (see photo 7 on the facing page). Then I apply more thinset and spread it with a ⅜-in. notched trowel. From this point, it becomes a typical tile installation.

Tom Meehan, a second-generation tile installer, and his wife, Lane, own Cape Cod Tileworks in Harwich, Massachusetts.

Easy to Install, Even over

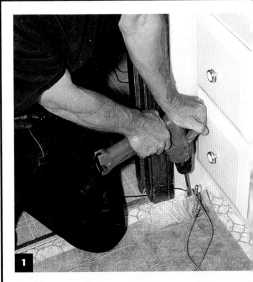

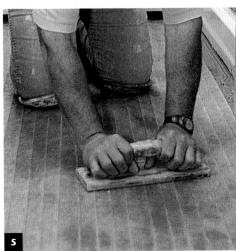

1. Locate the electrical feed. With the heat mat temporarily in place, the electrician drills in an inconspicuous spot to run wiring for the electrical feed and thermostatic control.

2. Don't rip it up, rough it up. The vinyl floor is roughed up so that the thinset will bond to it. The vinyl also serves as a slip sheet to prevent plywood seams from telegraphing through to the tile.

3. Use a ¼-in. notched trowel to spread the thinset. It's important to spread the thinset in one direction to allow the mat to sit evenly. Then unroll the mat at the door, pressing it into the thinset. Be careful not to work yourself into a corner while troweling thinset.

4. Unroll the mat, pushing it tight to keep it flat. Work the mat into the thinset, pressing it in while working forward. The wires in the mat are fragile, which is why setting it by hand is a good idea. The cabinets and fixtures are in place, making this installation easier.

5. Start from the middle and work your way out. To remove the voids or air pockets, a clean wood float does the trick. Be careful not to force the mat into place and possibly damage a connection.

6. Placing the sensor wire properly is critical. Once the mat is set, the electrician places the sensor wire. He will use strips of duct tape to hold it in place. It's important that the sensor wire doesn't cross the heating wires; otherwise, the thermostat won't get a proper reading.

7. Now it's a regular tile job. The thinset is troweled on with a ⅜-in. notched trowel with the trowel lines going in one direction. Take extra care when spreading thinset over the sensor wire. Once the tile is down, you might want to test the system. But wait a week for the thinset to cure before turning on the heat.

Garden Bathroom

■ ALAN JENCKS

In the closing segment of one of television's classic quiz shows, *What's My Line?*, a mystery guest would appear in silhouette, indistinct and not quite identifiable. Every morning, my client Judy saw a similar apparition in her bathroom mirror: a shadow outlined by the brilliantly illuminated south-facing window behind her.

Unpleasant lighting was just one of the problems in her old bathroom, which has doorways to a bedroom and a study. The bath is in an 1800-sq.-ft. Craftsman-style house built in 1908, but you wouldn't know it. The bathroom had suffered through at least two attempted upgrades, the most recent of which introduced a 1950s-era pinewood vanity cabinet into the décor. It ran most of the length of the north wall, leaving just enough space to open the study door about 40° (see the floor plan on p. 224). People unfamiliar with the room invariably bounced the door off the vanity when entering. This was our starting point.

Simple Changes, if Possible

I began by considering basic, inexpensive changes to the floor plan. But try as I might, the room resisted. One thing I absolutely didn't want to do was to relocate the doors, which would have meant tearing out perfectly good plaster, original moldings, built-in shelving, usable wall space, and various wiring circuits.

A box-bay window brings light into a bath that includes a sliding medicine cabinet and curved mahogany trim.

(15 in. from the center of the toilet to a finished wall).

This change left two problems to solve: one old and one new. First, the new bathtub is even wider than the pinewood vanity, so door clearance was still an issue. And second, the new pedestal sink I had in mind would be located beneath the window. Where would the mirror go?

The bathroom was getting more complex, and hence more expensive. But Judy agreed that a little more money well spent was better than a little less money poorly spent.

Finding Space in Surprising Places

To make enough room for the tub, I would have to annex the former linen-closet space, as well as expand into a portion of the closet in the study. But pushing the corner of the wall into the study's closet would render it largely useless. The solution was to curve the wall behind the tub, eliminating the sharp corner that would have impinged on the closet opening.

Initially, my design called for centering a mirror over the pedestal sink and surrounding it with a multilite window in an inverted U-shape. But I concluded that the upper windows would provide a view of only the underside of the roof overhang, thus putting the kibosh on that approach.

Another option was to gang three casement windows together and glaze the interior face of the center window with a mirror. This second idea would work, but it still felt wrong. I wanted to promote a greater feeling of spaciousness in the small room and bring in as much natural light as possible. Judy and I also wanted the option of turning the mirror into a medicine cabinet because storage space was already at a premium. These priorities led us to our eventual solution: a box-bay window with obscure glazing.

This window is similar to commercially available greenhouse windows, which have frames made of vinyl or aluminum and

A mobile medicine cabinet. The main mirror is mounted on a shallow mahogany cabinet that rides on a waxed rail in a corresponding groove. Windows at each end of the bay tilt inward, allowing screens to stay in place when windows are open for ventilation. Photos taken at A on floor plan (see p. 224).

To avoid the backlit-mirror condition, the locations of the tub and vanity needed to be switched. That made sense for another reason, too. Judy wanted a tub with a shower, so the window over the tub was a problem. Big exterior windows close to a moisture source such as a showerhead, even in our relatively mild Bay Area climate, inevitably lead to condensation that can grow mold and even damage the woodwork.

So a solution started to take shape: Swap the tub and vanity locations, and move the toilet the necessary 1½ in. out from the wall to comply with the building code

Rafter-Hung Bay Window

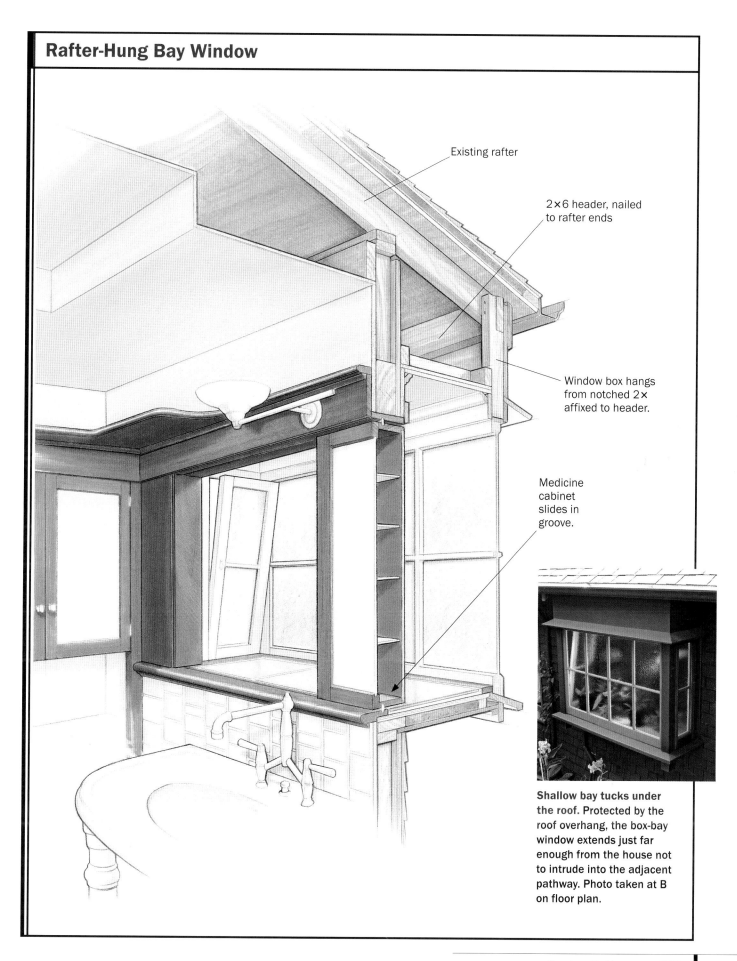

Existing rafter

2×6 header, nailed to rafter ends

Window box hangs from notched 2× affixed to header.

Medicine cabinet slides in groove.

Shallow bay tucks under the roof. Protected by the roof overhang, the box-bay window extends just far enough from the house not to intrude into the adjacent pathway. Photo taken at B on floor plan.

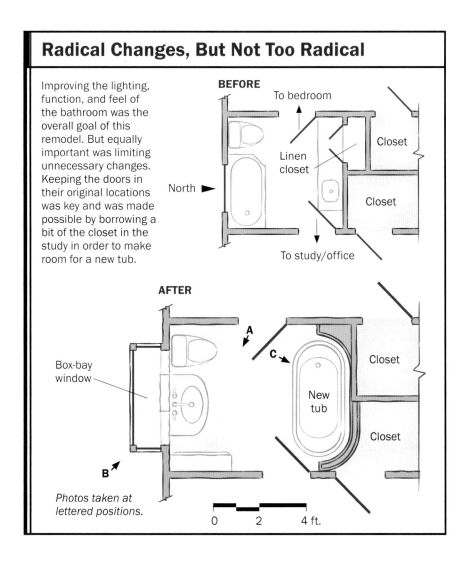

Radical Changes, But Not Too Radical

Improving the lighting, function, and feel of the bathroom was the overall goal of this remodel. But equally important was limiting unnecessary changes. Keeping the doors in their original locations was key and was made possible by borrowing a bit of the closet in the study in order to make room for a new tub.

BEFORE

To bedroom

Linen closet

Closet

North ▶

Closet

To study/office

AFTER

Box-bay window

A

C

Closet

New tub

Closet

B

Photos taken at lettered positions.

0   2   4 ft.

typically are topped with a shed roof. Judy's window is framed with wood and extends up the wall to be sheltered by the existing roof overhang (see the photo on p. 223).

For several reasons, a box-bay window turned out to be the right solution. First, moving the window about 16 in. beyond the plane of the wall increased the amount of glazing, and therefore daylight, in the room. It also had a large impact on the sense of space. At about 60 sq. ft., the bathroom is pretty modest in size. The deep window draws the eye toward the light and makes the space feel generous. The extra depth also made room for a sliding medicine cabinet in front of the window, freeing some space on the adjacent wall for a tall, thin storage cabinet.

I think the most important feature of the box window is Judy's garden. The bay has

turned out to be the ideal environment for her orchids, staghorn ferns, and violets. In addition to diffusing the light and affording a measure of privacy, obscure glass in the window keeps the focus on the plants, much the way stained-glass windows in a cathedral keep attention focused inward.

Mahogany Trim and High Shelves

Varnished or oiled woodwork is a hallmark of Craftsman-style houses. Here in the Bay Area, many of them are detailed with tight-grain old-growth redwood, a gorgeous wood that is in short supply and very expensive. I decided to use mahogany instead, which has the same rich color of redwood along with an extra measure of durability; it's much

Curved tub, curved wall. Instead of square corners behind the tub, curved ones minimized incursions into the closet space on the other side of the wall. Photo taken at C on floor plan.

Sources

Faucet and tub filler/wand:
Dornbracht, Madison tub filler
www.dornbracht.com

Lighting:
Metro Lighting, Chanterelle double sconce
www.metrolighting.com

Pedestal sink:
Whitehaus, model no. BTZ 34-GB001
www.whitehauscollection.com

Toilet:
Toto Clayton®
www.totousa.com

Trim and Shelves:
EarthSource Forest Products
www.earthsourcewood.com

Tub:
Porcher Époque®
www.porcher-us.com

harder than redwood, yet easy to work. I bought the mahogany, which came with Forest Stewardship Council certification, from EarthSource Forest Products®.

I used a quick-drying oil-based urethane finish called ProFin™ (www.dalyspaint.com) on the mahogany. This wipe-on finish is great for on-site applications when you don't have a spray booth and want to avoid brush strokes. One coat seals the wood but leaves a very open grain. You can add successive coats until you've got a mirrorlike semi-gloss surface, if that's what you're after.

A detail that consistently shows up in my work is a high shelf that runs around the room above the window and door headers. I'm not certain where my affection for this device originated, possibly from exposure to the intricate interiors of sailing ships and trains: small worlds where space is precious. These kinds of shelves inevitably become combination storage/display areas.

In Judy's bath, the 12-in.-deep shelves hold a row of rolled-up bath towels and a couple of fancy watering cans. The shelves are deep enough to feel a bit like soffits, adding a border of lower ceiling around the edges of the room. Over the pedestal sink, the shelves swoop back into the wall, making a curvy notch for the two-shaded wall sconce to splash light on the ceiling.

Alan Jencks is a residential designer specializing in remodels in Berkeley, California.

CREDITS

All photos are courtesy of *Fine Homebuilding* magazine (*FHb*) © The Taunton Press, Inc., except as noted below:

p. v: Photo by Charles Miller (*FHb*); p. vi: (left) Charles Miller (*FHb*), (right) Brian Pontolilo (*FHb*); p. vii: (left) Robert Yagid (*FHb*), (right) courtesy © Danze; p. viii: (left) Charles Miller (*FHb*), (right) Charles Bickford (*FHb*); p. 1: (left) Charles Miller (*FHb*), (right) Charles Miller (*FHb*).

p. 4: Bathroom Remodeling on Any Budget by Paul DeGroot, issue 207. All photos by Brian Pontolilo (*FHb*). All drawings by Martha Garstang Hill (*FHb*).

p. 19: The Perfect Master Bath by Stephen Vanze, issue 151. All photos by Charles Miller (*FHb*). All drawings by Sarah Walther (*FHb*).

p. 26: Two Approaches to the Basement Bath by Charles Miller, issue 207. All photos by Charles Miller (*FHb*) except photo on p. 28 courtesy © Greg Schmidt, and p. 31 courtesy © Paul Johnson. All drawings by Dan Thornton (*FHb*) except the drawings on p. 28 and p. 31 by Martha Garstang Hill (*FHb*).

p. 34: Closet or Bath? by Charles Miller, issue 191. All photos by Charles Miller (*FHb*) except photo on p. 34 courtesy © Leslie Lamarre. All drawings courtesy © Vince Babak.

p. 40: Two Baths from One by Genie Nowicki, issue 183. All photos by Brian Pontolilo (*FHb*) except photo on p. 42 courtesy © Harrell Remodeling. All drawings courtesy © Paul Perreault.

p. 46: Better Roof, Better Bath by Lisa Christie, issue 183. All photos by Charles Miller (*FHb*) except photo on p. 46 and p. 51 (bottom) courtesy © Jay Lane. All drawings courtesy © Paul Perreault.

p. 56: Plumbing a Basement Bathroom by Mike Guertin, issue 193. All photos by Chris Green (*FHb*) except p. 58 (bottom right) by Mike Guertin (*FHb*), p. 59 courtesy © Liberty Pumps, p. 60 and p. 62 by Charles Bickford (*FHb*), and p. 61 courtesy © Saniflo Inc. Drawing © courtesy John Hartman.

p. 64: Installing a Shower Niche by Jane Aeon, issue 196. All photos by Rob Yagid (*FHb*) except photo on p. 69 by Krysta S. Doerfler (*FHb*).

p. 70: Glass-Block Shower on a Curve by Tom Meehan, issue 120. All photos by Justin Fink (*FHb*) except photo on p. 70 courtesy © Tom Meehan, and photos on p. 74 by Krysta S. Doerfler (*FHb*).

p. 77: Shower-Door Sampler by Matthew Teague, issue 207. Photos on p. 77 and p. 85 by Robert Yagid (*FHb*); p. 78, p. 80 (bottom), and p. 81 courtesy © Basco; p. 79 courtesy © MTI; p. 80 (top) and pp. 82–84 courtesy © Kohler.

p. 86: Replace a Shower Mixing Valve by Ed Cunha, issue 176. Photo on p. 86 by Charles Bickford (*FHb*); pp. 87–91, and p. 92 (bottom left & right) courtesy © Tom Meehan (*FHb*); p. 92 (top photos) courtesy © Lane Meehan.

p. 93: Install a Pedestal Sink by Ed Cunha, issue 170. All photos © Tom Meehan except photos on p. 100 (left top & left bottom) courtesy © Kohler; and p. 100 (right top & right bottom) courtesy © Clawfoot Supply. Drawing by Dan Thornton (*FHb*).

p. 101: Buyer's Guide: Toilets by Nena Donovan Levine, issue 175. Photo on p. 101 courtesy © American Standard; p. 103 (top right) courtesy © Mansfield; p. 103 (bottom right) and p. 107 courtesy © Kohler; pp. 105–106 courtesy © Toto. Drawings by Don Mannes (*FHb*).

p. 108: Buyer's Guide: Bath Faucets by Patrick McCombe, issue 199. Photo on pp. 108–109 courtesy © Danze; p. 110 (left) courtesy © Delta; p. 110 (right) and p. 113 (bottom) courtesy © Kohler; p. 111 by Dan Thornton (*FHb*); p. 112 courtesy © California Faucets; p. 113 (top) courtesy © American Standard; p. 113 (middle) courtesy © Price Pfister; p. 114 (top) courtesy © Moen; p. 114 (bottom) courtesy © Niagara Conservation.

p. 115: Buyer's Guide: Bath Fans by Jefferson Kolle, issue 199. Photos on pp. 116–117 by Krysta S. Doerfler (*FHb*); pp. 118–119 photos by Brian Pontolilo (*FHb*). Drawings courtesy © Bob La Pointe.

p. 120: PEX Water Pipe: Is Copper on the Way Out by Andy Engel, issue 180. Photos on p. 121, p. 122 (bottom right), p. 123 (bottom), and p. 124 by Daniel S. Morrison (*FHb*); p. 122 (top and bottom left), and p. 123 (all top photos) by Krysta S. Doerfler (*FHb*); p. 126 and p. 128: courtesy © Vanguard. Drawings by Don Mannes (*FHb*).

p. 130: Preventing Moisture Problems in Bathrooms by Mary Jo Peterson, issue 151. Drawings courtesy © WOW House.

p. 140: A Sloping Floor for a Barrier-Free Bath by Tom Meehan, issue 185. All photos by Roe A. Osborn (*FHb*) except photo on p. 145 (bottom left), p. 146 (left photos), and p. 147 (top and middle) by Krysta S. Doerfler (*FHb*). Drawings courtesy © Clark Barre.

p. 150: Upgrading to a Tile Shower by Tom Meehan, issue 160. All photos by Roe A. Osborn (*FHb*) except photo on p. 150 (right) and p. 154 (top) by Charles Bickford (*FHb*); p. 154 (bottom photos) and p. 155 by Krysta S. Doerfler (*FHb*); p. 158 (left photos) courtesy © Lasco Bathware. Drawing by Dan Thornton (*FHb*).

p. 159: Putting the Craft Back in a Craftsman Bath by Jerri Holan, issue 159. All photos by Charles Miller (*FHb*) except inset photo on p. 161 courtesy © Jerri Holan.

p. 163: Glass Tile by Tom Meehan, issue 161. All photos by Charles Bickford (FHb) except photos on pp. 168–169 by Dan Thornton (*FHb*).

p. 171: Master Bath with a Twist by Chet Zebroski, issue 191. All photos by Charles Miller (*FHb*). All drawings courtesy © Vince Babak.

p. 175: A Skylight Cheers Up an Attic Bath by Scott Donahue, issue 199. All photos by Charles Miller (*FHb*). All drawings by Martha Garstang Hill (*FHb*).

p. 178: Brighten Up a Small Bath by Maaike Linnenkamp, issue 199. All photos by Charles Miller (*FHb*) except for photos on p. 181 courtesy © Maaike Linnenkamp. All drawings by Martha Garstang Hill (*FHb*).

p. 184: Install a Bathroom Fan by Mike Guertin, issue 157. All photos by Brian Pontolilo (*FHb*). Drawing on p. 185 by Don Mannes (*FHb*); p. 187 (left drawings) by Dan Thornton (*FHb*); p. 187 (right), p. 188, and p. 190 courtesy © Mark Hannon.

p. 192: Breathing Fresh Air into Bathroom Ventilation by Scott Gibson, issue 167. All photos by Scott Gibson (*FHb*) except middle right photo on p. 195 courtesy © American Aldes; p. 195 (bottom right), and p. 197 (top center) courtesy © Fantech. Drawing by Chuck Lockhart (*FHb*).

p. 198: Fight Mold with Paperless Drywall by Myron R. Ferguson, issue 210. All photos by Justin Fink (*FHb*) except photos on p. 198 and p. 202 (bottom right) by Dan Thornton (*FHb*).

p. 204: Cheaper Hot Water by Dave Yates, issue 199. Photo on p. 205 by Brian Pontolilo (*FHb*); p. 207 courtesy © Brian Leavitt; p. 212 courtesy © Dave Yates; p. 213 courtesy © John Morrison (*FHb*). All drawings courtesy © Jackie Rogers except for drawings on p. 209, p. 210 (bottom left), and p. 213 (top right) courtesy © John Hartman.

p. 214: Installing an Electric Radiant Floor by Tom Meehan, issue 159. Photo on p. 215 by Kevin Ireton (*FHb*); p. 216 and p. 218 (left photos) by Scott Phillips (*FHb*); p. 218 (right photos) and p. 219 by Roe A. Osborn (*FHb*). All drawings by © Bob La Pointe.

p. 220: Garden Bathroom by Alan Jenks, issue 159. All photos by Charles Miller (*FHb*). Drawing on p. 223 by Bob La Pointe; drawing on p. 224 courtesy © Paul Perreault.

INDEX

31901050914557